THE NAZIS
AND THE
SUPERNATURAL

THE NAZIS AND THE SUPERNATURAL

THE OCCULT SECRETS OF HITLER'S EVIL EMPIRE

MICHAEL FITZGERALD

This edition published in 2020 by Arcturus Publishing Limited
26/27 Bickels Yard, 151–153 Bermondsey Street,
London SE1 3HA

AD006669UK

Printed in the UK

CONTENTS

INTRODUCTION

Adolf Hitler's impact on the world is unprecedented and unparalleled. In twelve short years he left an indelible impact on history and the consequences of many of his actions continue to affect the world today. Even during his lifetime, he was as much a myth as a human being, and with the increasing distance of years his figure still fascinates to a unique degree. If anything, he has become even more like a cartoon villain than a real individual.

Following the defeat of Germany in the Second World War many people who had been enthusiastic Nazis rushed to denounce Hitler and to deny or minimize their own part in the regime. The safely dead Hitler and, to a lesser extent, Himmler were blamed for all the excesses and barbarity of the regime in a mass process of collective denial of guilt and individual responsibility that remains a unique phenomenon in human history.

There are several ways of interpreting historical events and processes and particularly the career of Hitler and the extraordinary period of the Nazi ascendancy. Hitler himself subscribed to Carlyle's 'great man' theory and saw himself as a heroic figure who had taken charge of the destiny of Germany and sought to place it on the path to greatness. Many of his contemporaries agreed with that estimate and broadly saw Hitler in those terms.

According to the Marxist interpretation of events, Hitler was simply a pawn who was manipulated into power to serve the interests of a desperate capitalist class and prevent the possibility of a Communist takeover in Germany. His policies were nothing more than capitalism applied with exceptional brutality and Hitler himself nothing more than a tool of big business. It was largely the level of unemployment within Germany that gave Hitler his chance.

Conservative interpretations of Hitler and the Nazis tend to stress the sense of national humiliation following the Treaty of Versailles, the occupation of the Ruhr and the shared sense of national failure. By giving Germans back a feeling of collective self-confidence, pride in their nation and themselves, a revived sense of community and the promise of renewed greatness, Hitler won their support and was able to make himself master of Germany.

In recent years what might be called 'technical' explanations have become more common. These theories stress the ability of Hitler and Goebbels to use propaganda, Hitler's power as a public speaker, the relative youth of the Nazi leadership and Hitler's cynical attempt to project an image of 'sex appeal' to women voters as the principal reasons for his success.

The culmination of Hitler's cult of personality: Albert Speer's 'Cathedral of Light' inspired a feeling of religious awe among those attending the Nuremberg Rally of 1936.

There are also various psychological explanations for Hitler's temporary triumph. His ability to tune in to the collective feelings of a nation, his capacity for rousing the emotions of a mass audience and his uncanny genius for diagnosing people's strengths and weaknesses have all been put forward to account for the Nazi phenomenon.

A variation of the psychological analysis approach is the range of theories putting forward an occult explanation for Nazism. Such ideas were first put forward as early as the 1930s, but it was with the astonishing success of Pauwels and Bergier's *The Morning of the Magicians* in the 1960s that they entered popular consciousness and became fashionable. A number of other writers followed their example, some engaging in a serious analysis of the extent to which occult factors did or did not play a significant part in the regime and others in little more than fantastic speculation.

There is of course some truth in all of the proposed explanations for Hitler's remarkable success. Without the dire economic position of Germany from 1929 to 1933 it is doubtful whether Hitler would ever have come to power. The sense of national humiliation within Germany was undoubtedly profound, but it could have been appealed to equally by a more conventionally nationalist politician as Stresemann demonstrated during the 1920s. The ability of Goebbels to manipulate public opinion through propaganda is also unquestionable as is Hitler's power as a rabble rouser and his awareness of and capacity for appealing to the collective feelings of a nation. All these factors certainly played an important part in his success, and yet the extent to which Nazism was a unique phenomenon remains. Stalin, Mao and other dictators were equally ruthless and homicidal, but even at their worst there was a core of logic behind their actions. Only Pol Pot among tyrants displayed the same degree of utter insanity and destructiveness, which is perhaps why he is the only dictator regarded with similar loathing.

Hitler's irrationality permeated every aspect of his life, his ideas and the manner in which Nazi Germany functioned once he came to power. His obsessional racism went far beyond simple prejudice and his policies of genocide continued until the last possible moment in spite of the far more urgent demands of the war. Hitler's frequently expressed contempt for rationality and science was hardly a helpful attitude in terms of restoring Germany to a position of greatness. His known belief in Hörbiger's Glacial Cosmogony was at least partly responsible for losing the war in Russia. During the final stages of the war he and Goebbels examined the horoscope of Germany to find a magical reprieve from defeat through the position of the stars in the heavens.

Many historians ignore, dismiss or downplay these aspects of Hitler and the regime. When faced with the exaggerated claims of some writers that Hitler and the Nazis were practising Satanists who were overwhelmingly motivated by occult considerations, it is difficult not to sympathize, but such an analysis of the Third Reich and its leader is not remotely plausible. On the other hand, to regard the occult aspects of the regime as of no importance or even as total fabrications is equally to be guilty of a flawed, superficial and inaccurate picture.

Occult factors and ideas undoubtedly entered into the thoughts and actions of Hitler and other Nazi leaders. They were certainly not the most important considerations in determining policy and decisions, but all the same they played a part.

The Nazi Occult War separates fact from fiction, myth from reality and examines to what extent occult factors affected Hitler and the Third Reich. The results of this analysis may well surprise both the fantasists and the doubters.

Chapter One
DARK INITIATES

THE TWELVE YEARS during which the Nazi Party ruled Germany and much of Europe were so fundamentally governed by irrational and even magical thinking that the whole period has sometimes been referred to as the 'occult Reich'. Hitler, Hess, Goering, Himmler, Bormann, Goebbels and Rosenberg were simply the most prominent believers in a way of thought that was entirely at odds with the secular thinking that had come to prevail in Europe. When the Third Reich was no more than a smouldering ruin, the Allied conquerors took a number of statements from Nazi Party members and discovered many documents about the way in which a range of occult notions had come to dominate the thinking of the most powerful leaders within Germany. They were so astonished by what they discovered that the evidence was deliberately suppressed at the Nuremberg Trials for fear that it would allow the defence lawyers to plead insanity on behalf of their clients.

How did it come about that Germany, a nation more closely identified than most with the spirit of rationality and enlightenment, had fallen under the control of a group of people who utterly rejected these views, preferring instead to follow the promptings of occultists and to espouse pseudo-scientific theories of race, superhuman beings and the virtue of genocide as a means of purifying Germany and eventually the world of the 'corruption' of 'inferior races'?

HITLER'S INTRODUCTION TO THE OCCULT

The trail begins six years before the commencement of the First World War. When the young Hitler was living in poverty in Vienna, he made friends with another dweller at the hostel for the homeless, Joseph Greiner. He introduced Hitler to a number of magical practices and showed him how to develop the power to control people and events. Hitler saw the new vistas that Greiner had shown him as offering the opportunity to escape from his present situation and translate his grandiose visions and ideas into reality through using the methods he had learned from his friend.

Hitler began studying hypnotism, yoga and other disciplines that he believed would help to strengthen his willpower. He attempted to move objects from a distance by focusing his will upon the exercise, and dowsed for water in the woods around Vienna. Hitler studied astrology, learning to draw up and cast a horoscope. He also learned numerology, graphology – assessing character from handwriting – and physiognomy – the art of judging people by their face and body language. Hitler sometimes tried to test the strength of his willpower by holding his hand under a burning gas jet. The fact that Greiner introduced Hitler to a number of occult practices is confirmed by others who knew him at the time, particularly Reinhold Hanisch who, like Greiner, shared a friendship with him at various doss-houses in Vienna.

LANZ AND ARYAN HEROES

In 1909, at the age of 20, Hitler met with Adolf Lanz, the head of an occult group based in Vienna. Lanz also published a newsletter called *Ostara*. Hitler regularly bought this paper from a local tobacconist's shop and met Lanz on a number of occasions, where he received further occult training. Lanz's newspaper and pamphlets first awakened Hitler's anti-Semitic prejudices, though they did not become fully formed until around 1920.

Lanz began his career as a Cistercian monk but was expelled from his monastery at the age of twenty-five for 'carnal and worldly

Hitler was presented to the German people as a man of mystical, supernatural power, able to reach out to them.

thoughts'. He immediately became an ardent German nationalist and a fierce anti-Semite who also attacked the Jesuits. Lanz also discarded the plain Herr Adolf Lanz to which he was entitled and began styling himself as Baron Jörg Lanz von Liebenfels. His occult group, the Order of the New Templars, was consciously modelled upon the Catholic Church.

Lanz set up centres for his Aryan heroes in various castles that he acquired for his order. By the 1920s they owned four castles, a house in Salzburg and a 'cell' in Hungary. He declared that 'the Aryan hero is on this planet the most complete incarnation of God and the spirit'. Unfortunately he had a bitter enemy known as the *Tschandala*, the underman. The *Tschandala* promoted democracy, capitalism and materialism. It was because the Aryan heroes had mixed their blood with apes that their race had degenerated. The Age of Aquarius would see the triumph of the newly racially purified Aryan over the sin of mingling his blood with that of lesser races.

The order laid down strict racial criteria for membership, including not simply blond hair and blue eyes but large heads, small hands and small feet. All those who joined his New Templars had to promise to marry racially pure women. Lanz claimed that 'through woman, sin came into the world, and it is so over and over again because woman is especially susceptible to the love artifices of her animal-like inferiors'.

The rather unedifying slogan of his order was 'race war until the castration knife'.

Lanz was also an obsessional advocate of nudism and devoted several issues of *Ostara* to the subject. He believed in a lost paradise where nude Aryans consorted in racially pure liaisons with Aryan women. The Fall came about through Aryan females breeding with 'the Dark Races' and Jesus (whom Lanz called Frauja) came to save them by issuing a new commandment 'love thy neighbour as thyself if he is a member of your own race'. He also denounced what he called 'inter-racial sexual relationships' and demanded forced labour and a starvation diet as punishment for these offences, calling for 'the extirpation of the animal-man and the propagation of the higher New Man' through selective breeding, sterilization, forced labour, transportation to 'the ape jungle' and even murder.

Lanz called his bizarre system of racial mythology Ariosophy and it involved a number of eccentric beliefs centred on the idea that when the Bible spoke of angels it meant 'Aryan heroes'. In his fantasies subhuman races emerged in the days of Atlantis and Lemuria. Lanz rejected the idea that humans had evolved from apes; his theories regarded apes as fallen men. Jews, Czechs and Slovenes were the three ethnic groups for whom he harboured particular hatred and in his eyes they had evolved through 'intermixing blood' between Aryans and apes. His Aryans were destined to be the Master Race and would lord it over inferior ethnic groups.

It is not for nothing that in 1932 Lanz wrote in a private letter to one of his students that 'Hitler is one of our pupils'. In 1934 he proudly claimed that his order was 'the first manifestation of National Socialism' and as late as 1951 he was still claiming to be the man who had inspired Hitler to adopt the Final Solution.

THE COSMIC CIRCLE OF MUNICH

Hitler was certainly influenced by Lanz's ideas but it was to be another six years or so before he began to formulate anything approaching a coherent ideology. When he moved to Munich in 1913, Hitler settled in the Schwabing area, the Bohemian quarter of the city. As well as mixing with other artists, he also discovered the ideas of Alfred Schuler and Ludwig Derleth. Schuler was convinced of the importance of what he called 'pure blood' and was strongly anti-Semitic. Both men belonged to a group that aspired to turn Munich into the centre of 'cosmic consciousness'. Their goal was to replace the existing political, social and religious structure of the world with 'the *Urheimat* [original home] of the soul'. They favoured instinctive rather than rational thinking, advocated following the promptings of the unconscious mind and tried to bring about a return to a more 'natural' and 'primitive' society.

Schuler revered the Roman Empire and blamed the Jews and Christians for its collapse. He engaged in séances, healing rituals and 'astral travel'. Schuler stressed the 'sacredness' of 'pure blood' and adopted the swastika as his personal symbol. Hitler heard Schuler lecture in Vienna and, as his friend Greiner related, developed an admiration for ancient Rome as a result. Schuler also led Hitler to become fascinated by the swastika symbol. He may have been a comparatively minor influence on the young Hitler but he reinforced his racial obsessions and gave him the most potent emblem of Nazism, the swastika.

Derleth subscribed to an even more bizarre belief system than Schuler. He was convinced that Schuler's séances were 'black magic rituals' and his own megalomania soon led to his notorious *Proclamations*, in which he declared the imminent arrival of 'Christus Imperator Maximus'. This coming saviour of the world wanted 'death-hardened troops for the conquest of the globe'. The last sentence of the *Proclamations* became notorious: 'soldiers, I deliver unto you for plundering – the

JOSEPH GREINER

STARB
HIER
AM
2·1·36
. DEN
FIEBERTOD
IM
DIENSTE
DEUTSCHER
FORSCHUNGS
ARBEIT

DEUTSCHE
AMAZONAS
JARY
EXPEDITION
1935·37

„Rätsel der Urwaldhölle"

Researching the Amazon's potential as a future German colony, Joseph Greiner visited the rainforest in 1935 but succumbed a year later to fever and was buried there.

world!' His 'Reich of Christ the king' found few disciples but his ideas were widely publicized in Munich and were mentioned favourably by the *Schwabinger Beobachter*, the newspaper of the local Bohemian community.

Hitler was aware of Derleth's *Proclamations* and of his project for the establishment of the *Rosenburg*, his vision of an ideal city. The *Rosenburg*, though never more than a dream, was favourably commented upon by Lanz and other thinkers who influenced the young Hitler. It was also an ideal that Himmler found attractive when he came to consider his own vision of the Utopian state over which he imagined his SS (*Schutzstaffel*) ruling in the event of final German victory. Derleth's fascination with alchemy, organic farming, living in harmony with nature, vegetarianism, 'spiritual development' and an 'order' that created and ruled a 'golden society' were decisive influences upon Himmler's conception of the world.

THREE MEN WHO CHANGED THE COURSE OF HITLER'S LIFE

In 1919 Hitler met three men in Munich who, more than any others, profoundly shaped his thought and laid the foundations of his political career. All three were deeply involved in occult practices. The influence of Gottfried Feder, Dietrich Eckart and Alfred Rosenberg proved decisive in transforming him into the future leader of Germany.

It began when Hitler attended a talk at the German Workers' Party on 12 September 1919. The speaker was Feder and the subject of his talk was capitalism and its evils. There were only fifty-four members of the party, few of them present that evening. Hitler listened to Feder's talk with fascination and was strongly attracted to the new economic ideas that he put forward. During the questions that followed the speaker's lecture, a member of the audience demanded that the state of Bavaria should secede from the rest of Germany and restore its former monarchy.

Hitler stood up angrily and engaged in a passionate defence of a Greater Germany that included not only the states that already belonged to it but also Austria, Danzig and all of the German-speaking

The swastika was an auspicious symbol in Tibet. This photo was taken by Ernst Schäfer in Lhasa, 1938/9

peoples. Having made his statement he was about to make a rapid exit when the party leader, Anton Drexler, rushed after him and managed to get his address. He left the meeting but received a membership card in the post the following day.

Drexler and Feder were both deeply impressed with Hitler's charisma, speaking ability and strength of conviction. As Drexler remarked after hearing Hitler speak, 'My God, he's got the gift of the gab, hasn't he? We could use him.'

As a result of the meeting Hitler became the fifty-fifth member of the German Workers' Party and the seventh member of its committee, given special responsibility for propaganda. Before long it had been renamed the National Socialist German Workers' Party and Hitler became its leader. He was to transform it into a mass movement, using to a considerable extent the occult training he had received from the dark initiates of the Thule Group and the Vril Society.

Very few of the ideas that the future Chancellor of Germany put forward during his political career were original. His economic policies were almost entirely derived from Feder and his anti-Semitism, still a relatively vague and incoherent prejudice before he met them, hardened into dogma as he swallowed the occult-based racial theories of Eckart and Rosenberg. Unlike Hitler all three men came from wealthy middle-class families and they decisively changed the direction of Hitler's life and as a result the future history of the world through their ability to provide a more sophisticated 'justification' for prejudices that however deeply felt had perhaps not been clearly formulated before.

DIETRICH ECKART – HITLER'S SPIRITUAL FATHER

Eckart knew that the German Workers' Party, even though he shared its beliefs, was incapable of ever becoming a mass movement without the right sort of person as its leader. He said in the spring of 1919 before he had met Hitler, 'we need a man at the head who can stand the sound of a machine gun. The best man for the job would be a worker who knows how to talk'.

Eckart was obsessed with the imminent arrival of a strong leader who would not only restore Germany to its former greatness but would make it the most powerful nation on earth. He was immediately struck by Hitler's potential and became convinced that the young Austrian ex-corporal was the Messiah for whom he and the whole of Germany were waiting. Hitler was not from the upper or middle classes, so he had the ability to speak to the working classes as one of their own. His charisma and ability as a public speaker was beyond question. Eckart believed that Hitler could be moulded into the future saviour of Germany with sufficient training by himself and others who shared his own view of the world.

Eckart nurtured Hitler carefully and initiated him into a range of occult ideas and practices. He introduced him to three magical orders: the Thule Group, the Armanen Order and the Vril Society. From them Hitler learned the techniques of occult concentration, of visualization and of developing the power to direct his will to influence events and other people.

Eckart firmly believed that he was in contact with the 'Secret Chiefs', mysterious beings who were variously thought to live in the air, in the mountain fastnesses of Tibet or in the very centre of the earth. He thought he had the power to summon them and set them to work on behalf of Germany and that Hitler was the earthly instrument for channelling their power.

Kurt Ludecke was a close friend of Hitler for many years and described Eckart as 'something of a genius, and to a great degree the spiritual father of Hitler and the grandfather of the Nazi movement'. For his part Eckart told Rosenberg, 'Let it happen as it will and must, but I believe in Hitler; above him there hovers a star.'

Like Feder, Eckart was deeply hostile to capitalism. Feder, at least at first, did not regard his anti-capitalist views as being necessarily connected with anti-Semitism but Eckart believed firmly that the Jews were the masterminds behind capitalism. Through his newspaper *Auf gut Deutsch* and his authorship of a number of pamphlets, particularly the incendiary *To All Workers!*, he built a following among the thousands of Germans who felt dispossessed and alienated at the end of the First World War. Under Eckart's influence, first Feder and then Hitler came to look on the Jews as the source of all the evils in the world.

THE THULE GROUP

The very beginnings of Nazism were steeped in occultism. The Nazi Party began life as the political arm of the Thule Group. This was founded in 1910 by Felix Niedner who also translated the *Eddas* from Old Norse into German. (The *Eddas* were the sacred books of Scandinavian paganism.) In 1918 a Munich branch was founded and became involved in political activity.

The Thule Group was formed on the ancient myths of Hyperborea and Thule. Hyperborea was supposed to be a land in the far north that was destroyed by ice. The ice split it into two islands, one of which

The emblem of the Thule Group, an amalgamation of occultists whose beliefs centred on the coming of a 'German Messiah', the 'Great One', who would restore Germany to its former glory after the humiliation of defeat in the First World War

became known as Thule. The Thule Group members were convinced that their descendants were the ancestors of the Aryan race.

The group was one of the most important formative influences on Nazi thinking. Only the Vril Society had an equally decisive impact on the Party's leadership.

Eckart was also obsessed with the idea of the *Reichskleinodien*, the treasures of the Holy Roman Empire, in particular the crown and sceptre that had been part of the regalia of successive emperors. He was particularly keen on transferring the ownership of the Spear of Destiny to the possession of a Greater German Reich.

In spite of his total hostility to both Christianity and Judaism, Eckart was convinced that it was essential for the Nazis to acquire as many as possible of the sacred relics of both religions in order to harness their power. It was also Eckart who introduced Hitler to

The imperial regalia of the emperors and kings of the Holy Roman Empire, dating from the Middle Ages, constitute one of the most important collections of royal jewels.

the bizarre writings of the anti-Semitic Jew Otto Weininger, which provided additional occult justification for Aryan supremacism and anti-Jewish attitudes.

OTTO WEININGER: THE ANTI-SEMITIC JEW

Weininger was a Jewish psychologist who was deeply ashamed of his Jewishness. Like most thinkers of his generation he believed that ethnic and national differences were inherent rather than culturally determined. In his book *Sex and Character* Weininger divided countries into what he referred to as 'masculine' and 'feminine' nations. People from the Mediterranean areas were regarded as female and northern Europeans as male. In the same way he claimed that nations and racial groups were 'active' or 'passive'. Again masculine nations were active and feminine ones passive. Naturally Weininger saw the Germans as active and the Jews as passive.

Not content with this dubious classification of nations and ethnic groups, Weininger added sexism to his racial prejudices. Women were condemned utterly as materialistic, passive and feminine while men were spiritual, active and masculine. His suggestion that women were less spiritual than men represented a complete reversal of orthodox attitudes towards gender and spirituality.

The core of Weininger's book was a polemic against feminine values and women in general. His notorious remark 'the best woman is inferior to the worst man' summed up his attitude towards them. Women were not only seen as inferior to men but also as not even fully human at all. They had no value in themselves and only acquired an instrumental value in terms of their ability to serve men.

Weininger further declared that Jews were inferior even to women since women believed in men but Jews believed in nothing. Jews were completely unable to live their lives upon spiritual principles and were the incarnation of the spirit of decadent materialism. This tendency made them the natural enemies of the German people. Weininger wrote:

The human race awaits the founder of a new religion and the struggle approaches its crucial phase, as in the first year of our era. Once again humanity has the choice between Judaism and Christianity, between commerce and culture, between woman and man, between the species and the individual, between non-value and value, between nothingness and divinity; there is no third kingdom.

As with Hitler and many other Nazis Weininger saw race not simply in biological terms but also as representing spiritual values. He declared that Judaism was 'a tendency of the intellect, a psychic condition which could appear in any man but whose greatest historical manifestation was in historical Judaism'. Weininger also believed that the German race represented the highest expression of spiritual values.

This tormented, self-hating Jew influenced thinkers of the stature of Wittgenstein and Freud. For all the irrationality of his prejudices against women and Jews he roundly condemned anti-Semitism and wrote:

The most genuine Aryans, those who are most Aryan and most sure of their Aryanism are not anti-Semites. On the other hand, in the aggressive anti-Semite one can always detect certain Jewish traits even though his blood is free from any Semitic strain. That is why the most violent anti-Semites are Jews.

A year after converting to Christianity Weininger committed suicide. His work *Sex and Character* was a popular and influential book that was widely praised. Two of its biggest admirers were Eckart and Alfred Rosenberg, a man whose decisive influence upon Hitler will be examined shortly. Eckart introduced Hitler to Weininger's book and the future Chancellor was deeply impressed. In his *Table Talk*, Hitler described Weininger as 'the only Jew fit to live'.

Otto Weininger: 'the only Jew fit to live' – Hitler.

ALFRED ROSENBERG, THE NAZI PARTY IDEOLOGIST

Rosenberg found Weininger's attitudes towards women as congenial as his racist fantasies. He declared that men thought 'systematically' while women thought 'lyrically'; male thinking was 'synoptic' while females thought 'atomistically'. Rosenberg believed that the principal role of women was 'to preach the maintenance of the purity of the race'.

In Rosenberg's eyes the growing emancipation of women was a disastrous mistake. He rejected absolutely any notion of the equality of the sexes which he identified with liberal values that in his view had nearly destroyed Germany. Rosenberg believed that the whole notion of human rights was not simply an illusion but a dangerous mistake. Biology had created two genders and the differences between men and women were innate rather than cultural. Women were inferior to men and only through restoring the natural order of things with male headship and female subservience could the errors of feminism, 'artificially created by an intellectualism of the most depraved kind', be overcome and reversed. The role of a woman was to preserve the race, to maintain domestic virtue and uphold morality. Feminism was 'a symptom of decay' and 'invented by the Jewish intellect' to try and destroy the Aryan race.

In 1919 Eckart introduced Hitler to Rosenberg and his influence upon Hitler's ideology was decisive. Rosenberg was obsessed with anti-Semitism, anti-Communism, anti-capitalism, anti-Freemasonry and anti-Christianity, as well as having a deep hatred of lesbianism and a bizarre compulsion to collect musical instruments. He not only believed in the Thulean origin of the Aryan race but was also firmly committed to 'the creation of a new human type' that would dominate 'subhuman races' and move humanity on to a 'higher plane' through occult methods.

Both Eckart and Rosenberg believed in a very strange kind of religion. On the whole, the ancient pagan faiths had worshipped natural forces and had believed firmly in the importance of making life on earth as happy as possible. These two men were convinced that the material world was not simply illusory but evil. They saw it as the duty of the human race to seek to evolve into a level where it would be able to live on a 'non-material plane of existence'.

Alfred Rosenberg was important in shaping Nazi ideology. He rejected Christianity as being a Jewish religion and formalized a hierarchy of races with Aryans at the top.

THE PROTOCOLS OF THE LEARNED ELDERS OF ZION

Rosenberg had lived in Estonia when it was still part of Russia. The Bolshevik Revolution forced him to flee and he lost all his wealth. When he arrived in Germany as a penniless refugee he had only one 'weapon' in the attempt to regain his former privileged status. This was a copy of the notorious *Protocols of the Learned Elders of Zion*, a work that claimed to be an account of the secret proceedings of the World Congress of Jewry held at Basel in 1897 and which allegedly laid down plans for world Jewish domination.

Rosenberg knew perfectly well that the *Protocols* were a forgery but he also realized their potentially explosive effect if they were widely disseminated. After reading *Auf gut Deutsch* he went to see Eckart and presented him with the manuscript of the *Protocols*. A tremendously excited Eckart arranged for their publication in a German translation. He also invited Rosenberg to join the Thule Group and later introduced him to Hitler. Rosenberg arrived in Munich in November 1918 and joined the German Workers' Party in January 1919. Hitler did not become a member until October 1919.

Rosenberg did not publish his ideas in book form immediately. Instead he began by writing articles for Eckart's newspaper. In late 1919 he completed his first full-length manuscript, *The Trace of the Jew Through Changing Times*. In this bizarre, rambling and often incoherent work he claimed that the colours of the new national flag introduced by the Weimar Republic (red, black and gold) represented three different aspects of the alleged 'Jewish High Command' and their goal of 'world domination'. In Rosenberg's paranoid imagination red stood for 'Jewish Bolshevism', black for 'Jewish anarchism' and gold for 'Jewish High Finance'. He said that 'the black, the red and the gold internationals represent the dreams of Jewish philosophers from Ezra, Ezekiel and Nehemiah to Marx, Rothschild and Trotsky'. He also declared that not only was Freemasonry yet another 'front' for the conspiracy but that England, 'the land where Freemasonry originates', was 'the centre of world Jewry'.

The Freemasons had been accused of political involvement by conspiracy theorists for around two hundred years but it appears to have been Rosenberg's particular contribution to declare firmly that it was a specifically 'Jewish' conspiracy. In his second book, *The Crime of the Freemasons*, he engaged in a tirade against 'Jewish Masonry'.

He soon converted Eckart and Hitler to his way of thinking and within a surprisingly short time it had become the orthodox view among far-right movements. Rosenberg himself was appointed to the position of the Party's official ideologist. His job was to provide 'facts' to support the various claims made by its spokesmen. He also played a large part in formulating the basic 'philosophy' of Nazism.

Another two books followed before his edition of the *Protocols* became an international publishing sensation. Rosenberg added an extensive commentary on the work and prepared the book for the press.

As he had hoped and expected, the effect of the *Protocols* was immediate and worldwide. They launched an international anti-Semitic movement and even though *The Times*, which had begun by taking them seriously, was able comparatively quickly to demonstrate that the work was a forgery, the *Protocols* became an integral part of anti-Jewish propaganda employed by the far right.

Hitler of course became totally convinced of the genuineness of the *Protocols* in spite of the fact that even Rosenberg knew they were a forgery. In the first German edition of the work Rosenberg had carefully stated that 'as matters stand today it is impossible to adduce juridically conclusive proof either for their absolute authenticity or for their fabrication'. When he came to write *Mein Kampf* Hitler declared that they were not only genuine but that they also showed clear proof of a Jewish conspiracy against the world.

THE MYTH OF THE 20TH CENTURY

Adding to the huge influence that his introduction of the *Protocols* to Germany had wrought upon Hitler and the Nazis, Rosenberg also worked on his most ambitious book, *The Myth of the 20th Century*. It finally saw publication in 1930 and was the second most popular Nazi work after *Mein Kampf*, selling over a million copies. Even Hitler described it as the most important formulation of Nazi policy other than his own work.

It has become fashionable to underrate Rosenberg's influence upon Hitler. Certainly for the last three years of the war he was relatively ineffective, but that was far from being the case for the majority of his political career. Hitler thought so highly of him that following his own arrest after the failed Munich Putsch in 1923 he appointed Rosenberg as Party leader, a position he retained until Hitler's eventual release.

When the Nazis came to power Rosenberg enjoyed authority over a wide range of activities, hardly a sign of incapacity or of being undervalued by the leadership. While never in the same class as Goebbels, Himmler, Bormann or Heydrich as an administrator, he still succeeded in having more of his policies carried out than the majority of Nazi leaders. The enormous influence that Rosenberg had on the Führer's thinking is demonstrated constantly by Hitler in *Mein Kampf*, in *Table Talk*, in many of his speeches and in the various conversations he had with other people, particularly those recorded by Hermann Rauschning, Governor of Danzig. Rosenberg was sometimes referred to as 'the keeper of the faith' or 'the conscience of the Party'. However incoherent and repellent his ideas may appear today, they had a profound influence on the Nazis and particularly upon Hitler.

In *The Myth of the 20th Century* Rosenberg claimed that materialism and individualism were dying creeds and that they would become submerged into the group identity of the *Volk*. He believed that Atlantis lay in the far north and was the original home of the Aryans. Rosenberg also denounced Catholicism with considerable venom and praised what he called the 'martyrs of free research'. In his mind these included 'the Albigenses, Waldenses, Cathars, Arnoldists, Stedingers, Huguenots and reformed Lutherans'. This suspiciously miscellaneous assortment of religious dissenters had almost nothing in common with one another beside the fact that they all fell foul of the Catholic Church.

The Huguenots and Lutherans disagreed with each other on almost every issue; the Waldenses attracted persecution for their attacks on wealth and privilege rather than for any significant doctrinal issues with Catholicism; the Arnoldists and Stedingers were obscure and of no real significance; and the Cathars were identical with the Albigenses.

It is not surprising that Rosenberg's hatred of materialism led him to lavish his greatest praise on the Cathars. Like them he saw the physical world as evil and something from which we should all seek to escape. In Rosenberg's eyes the spirit is trapped in the material universe and only through the renunciation of the world can it become free. To him the true purpose of mysticism was to enable humans to evolve beyond their physical bodies and life on earth and to enter the higher realm of the purely spiritual existence.

By contrast Rosenberg believed the Jews were the arch-materialists, totally committed to life upon earth and a 'worldly' view of human behaviour. He denounced Judaism and the Jews as 'enemies of the spirit' and in a passage extraordinary even by his standards declared that 'to strip the world of its soul, that and nothing else is what Judaism wants. This, however, would be tantamount to the world's destruction'.

In *The Myth of the 20th Century* Rosenberg examined the Cathars in considerable detail. He made his admiration for their beliefs plain and in particular saw their version of Christianity as superior to that of the Catholic Church. Rosenberg saw Catholicism as a corruption of the Christian religion and believed the Cathars were the guardians of true Christianity. In his eyes, although Luther and Calvin had been right to condemn the Catholic Church their criticisms of it had not gone far enough.

Both Luther and Calvin believed in the literal truth of the Bible as the revealed word of God and reverenced the Old Testament at least as much as the New. By contrast the Cathars rejected the entire Old Testament and much of the New Testament as well.

Rosenberg saw St Paul as another tool of the vast Jewish conspiracy. In his eyes Paul had realized that Christianity was spreading and was threatening to replace Judaism. Paul was therefore sent by the rabbis to corrupt it. If it had not been for Paul, Christianity would have lost its Jewish elements and would have been an anti-Semitic religion more or less along the lines of Catharism.

Rosenberg denounced Christianity for its failure to recognize the inherent superiority and inferiority of the world's various ethnic groups. He rejected the idea of original sin and declared that the Germans were 'born noble'. He also condemned its belief in personal immortality. Rosenberg never made entirely plain what alternative view he held on the question of human survival of death, but almost certainly his own preference was for the theory of reincarnation.

ROSENBERG AND THE BASIS OF NAZI LAW

As the Party's official ideologist, Rosenberg laid down the basis for German state law. He proclaimed that the *Volk*, the people of the blood, constituted the state. It was the membership of this community of the *Volk* that determined the thoughts and actions of all Germans. Any conflicting loyalties could not be admitted, whether to churches or rival political parties. The unity of the people under the leadership of the *Führer* demanded an absolute denial of individual liberty of conscience. Instead the only permitted form of thought was National Socialism. Society consisted simply of people of the same racial type and that alone defined their place. The individual had no meaning or existence outside the *Volk*.

The Catholic Church certainly saw Rosenberg as a serious enemy. In the papal encyclical *Mit brennender Sorge* ('With Burning Concern') the Pope specifically denounced *The Myth of the 20th Century*. Apart from the comparative rarity of a papal attack on a particular book it was also unusual at that time for an encyclical to be written and published in German.

During the early years of the Nazi Party Rosenberg became the editor of its newspaper, the *Völkischer Beobachter* ('People's Observer'), and used his position to promote and popularize his own ideology. In

1934 Hitler rewarded his years of service by appointing him to the post of *Beauftragter des Führers für die Überwachung der gesamten geistigen und weltanschaulichen Schulung und Erziehung der Partei und gleichgeschalteten Verbände.* This title is almost untranslatable, the closest English equivalent being 'the *Führer's* representative for the oversight of the entire spiritual and ideological education and instruction of the Party and incorporated groups'.

ROSENBERG AND MODERN ART

Rosenberg used his new position to intervene in a range of areas – schools, youth groups, political ideology, social issues, religion, literature and the arts. When Hitler came to power Rosenberg set up the National Socialist Community of Culture. By 1935 it had over one and a half million members. The Community organized circles for art, books, theatre and lectures with a membership fee of one mark per circle. The theatre division of the organization read over three thousand manuscripts a year. Literature, art and music all had to reflect what Rosenberg called 'a definite view of the world'. He demanded an end to 'the philosophy of democratic levelling' and insisted upon the primacy of 'unspoiled instincts as against the speculative theorems of hollow fancies'. Cultural activity was seen as a means of organizing 'receptivity of the ear, the eye and the heart for the great masters of works of German art' which would create 'a cultural works community'.

Rosenberg was bitterly hostile towards modern art which he saw as degenerate and yet another example of the Jewish conspiracy. One of his first acts on achieving power was to denounce the world-famous *Bauhaus* and it closed shortly afterwards. Rosenberg demanded that all true art should be *völkisch* and express a collective sense of community and in particular celebrate rural life. In 1934 he closed an exhibition of experimental artists and aspired to be the cultural dictator of Germany. This ambition brought him into conflict with Goebbels.

Temperamentally, ideologically and in terms of their abilities, the two men could hardly have been more different. Rosenberg was shy, a poor speaker, a romantic traditionalist, a man who found it hard to relate to other people and was completely lacking in a sense of humour. Goebbels was extroverted, a brilliant speaker, a modernist, a man who was known for his biting wit and who was nearly always able to persuade people to adopt his point of view. With both men set on determining ideological orthodoxy and the cultural direction of the Reich it was inevitable that they would clash. Given Goebbels' ability to think on his feet, his vastly superior organizational ability, his genius for propaganda and total lack of scruples, it was also inevitable that the remote conservative intellectual Rosenberg would lose the power struggle between them.

In spite of his overall failure to control the cultural side of German life, it was largely Rosenberg who was responsible for the wholesale condemnation of modern art. Goebbels and Goering both championed artistic modernism enthusiastically and Hitler, at least during the 1920s, had also been sympathetic to many aspects of modern art. Under Rosenberg's influence the Nazi Party condemned it in its totality and the notorious 1937 exhibition of 'degenerate art' was almost entirely his idea. It backfired spectacularly, drawing huge crowds, but after its closure artists found themselves forced to follow the official party line of representationalism in art. Once again Rosenberg had persuaded Hitler to change the direction of party policy.

Rosenberg's principal influence was through the educational sections of the Nazi Party and his impact both on the content and style of the training for future Party leaders was undeniable. An impressive variety of literature was prepared by his office including the *Bulletin on the Doctrinal Situation* and *Idea and Deed*. The latter publication contained 'teaching materials for the entire doctrinal education of the NSDAP' and a 'bibliography for the work of doctrinal education'. Another important Rosenberg publication was the *National Socialist Monthly* which was the principal political and cultural journal of the Party. Rosenberg was also given responsibility for creating the *Lebensfeiern* – the ceremonies designed to replace religious rites of baptism, marriage and funerals.

GOTTFRIED FEDER AND NAZI ECONOMIC PHILOSOPHY

If Rosenberg's influence on Hitler has been grossly underrated, particularly before 1941, Feder is an almost forgotten figure nowadays, tending to attract no more than a brief mention in footnotes or at best a paragraph or two. In spite of his present obscurity, Feder's influence upon Hitler's thinking was every bit as profound as that of Rosenberg or Eckart. Like them, Feder belonged to the Thule Group and the Vril Society. It was Feder who spoke at the first meeting of the future Nazi Party that Hitler attended. Feder introduced Hitler to Eckart and Feder's economic ideas captivated Hitler and became Party policy. It was Feder who drew up the 'unalterable' 25-point programme of the Nazi Party. When the socialist wing of the Party rebelled against Hitler, Feder was the man chosen to put down the revolt.

From the moment they met, Feder became not simply an adviser to Hitler but a close personal friend. He was so excited by Hitler's brief intervention at the Party meeting that he told Eckart he believed the movement had found the leader it was looking for. It was Feder who convinced Hitler that a nationalist form of socialism was possible and, at least indirectly, was responsible for the choice of the name 'National Socialist German Workers' Party'.

Writing about the talk by Feder which set him on the beginning of his political career, Hitler remarked:

> *After hearing the first lecture delivered by Feder, the idea immediately came into my head that I had found a way to one of the most essential prerequisites for the founding of a new party. I understood immediately that here was a truth of transcendental importance for the future of the German people. In Feder's speech I found an effective rallying cry for our coming struggle.*

Bavarian Gottfried Feder was a member of the Thule Group and a founder of the DAP. In February 1920, he was architect of the '25 points', a statement of the original Nazi agenda

Feder was the least inclined towards the occult of all Hitler's mentors, possibly because of his background as an engineer. He was certainly as hostile to 'materialism' as Hitler or Eckart and Rosenberg and to a considerable extent they persuaded him that 'high finance' – what would nowadays be referred to as 'global capitalism' or 'financial capitalism' – was being masterminded by the Jews. Feder said on 27 June 1920 that it

> was not a question of race. Obviously however the Jewish question is concerned with the solution of the problem, for representatives of Jewry stand in the first line of attack.

Even in 1933 when the Nazis were in power Feder declared that 'Jewry' represented 'the spirit of materialism' and that was why it was directly opposed to the abolition of 'interest slavery'.

For all his intense hatred of materialism and his frequent tirades against the Jews, Feder did not subscribe to the global anti-Semitic views of his leader and the majority of his colleagues in the Nazi Party.

All of these men were part of the intellectual influences that helped form the essential thinking of the future *Führer*. Hitler had been exposed to a range of magical and occult views from the age of nineteen until the day he became German Chancellor and it is hardly surprising that once he came to power he set out to put as many of his esoteric theories into practice as possible, with consequences that affected the subsequent development of the whole world and in many respects continue to do so to the present day.

Chapter Two

THE VRIL SOCIETY

FOLLOWING GERMANY'S DEFEAT in the First World War the country erupted into revolution. The Kaiser fled abroad, seeking sanctuary in neutral Holland. There was a huge swing to the left politically and the Social Democratic Party provided the new republic with its President and its first Chancellor.

In this time of crisis political extremism flourished and threatened to push the country into full-scale civil war. Inspired by Lenin's success in Russia, the German Communists attempted to install a similar regime in their own country. Disillusionment with the political establishment was so intense that ordinary ideological boundaries collapsed or became at least blurred. Only the aristocrats and the wealthy still believed in the monarchy and the rule of an elite.

Large numbers of demobilized soldiers roamed aimlessly across the country. They found themselves despised and hated by the population and became resentful and bitter as a result. Many ex-soldiers joined the revolutionaries and formed 'Soldiers' Councils'. Others joined nationalist paramilitary groups known as *Freikorps* – Free Corps.

At this time of upheaval within Germany two of the men who were to create and shape the destiny of the Third Reich chose very different courses of action. Captain Ernst Röhm formed one of the most effective *Freikorps* units. Corporal Adolf Hitler by contrast joined the Marxist revolutionaries and was an active and enthusiastic supporter of the brief but violent 'Soviet Bavaria' regime. He was even elected as a member of one of the 'Soldiers' Councils' in Munich.

As well as the predictable political groupings of communists, socialists, liberals and conservatives, some more eccentric attempts to remould society also sprang up and flourished briefly. There was an astonishing overlap of ideas and personnel between many of these groups, particularly the radical right and the far left.

Feder observed the political and financial ruin of his country and developed his own ideas for a solution to its economic problems. He began by approaching German bankers with his proposals but was rebuffed. His next step was to present a 'Manifesto for the abolition of the interest-slavery of money' to the Marxist government of Soviet Bavaria on 20 November 1918. It is highly significant that Feder saw no inherent contradiction between approaching bankers and Communists with identical proposals for economic reform.

The following year Feder, after reading *Auf gut Deutsch*, met with the paper's editor and chief writer, Eckart. They became close friends and before long Eckart had recruited Feder into the Thule Group and the Vril Society.

The Vril Society has been mentioned briefly already but it is worthy of extended consideration. Unlike Feder, whose politics were always essentially on the left, Eckart's views were confused, contradictory and irrational. Where Feder saw the hand of 'high finance' Eckart saw 'an international Jewish conspiracy'. Feder wanted a return to spiritual values; Eckart believed that this could only be achieved through a determined opposition to 'Judah'.

The original Vril Society had been small and ineffective. The Munich branch, founded by Rudolf von Sebottendorf, was a very

Victory parade at Nuremberg in 1933, featuring Hitler and his head pitbull Ernst Röhm in SA uniform. Röhm was a hyperactive member of the Freikorps movement.

different organization. As early as 9 November 1918, two days before the war ended and while the Kaiser still sat on the throne of Germany, Sebottendorf denounced what he called 'a revolution made by a lower race to corrupt Germans', adding 'we are now confronted by our mortal enemy – Judah'.

THE BEGINNINGS OF THE NAZI PUBLISHING EMPIRE

In July 1918 Sebottendorf bought a publishing house and a newspaper. The publishers, Franz Eher Verlag, later issued many Nazi books. The newspaper was renamed the *Münchener Beobachter und Sportsblatt*. Later it was rebranded as the *Völkischer Beobachter* and became the official organ of the Nazi Party.

In his newspaper Sebottendorf called for a counter-revolution against the left-wing regime. He also founded a 'workers' ring' in November 1918 to try and counter Marxist ideas among the working classes. Membership of the ring – the *Politischer Arbeiterzirkel* (Workers' Political Circle) was derisory. Other than Sebottendorf himself, the only regular members were Karl Harrer, a sports reporter; Anton Drexler, a railway worker; and two of Drexler's fellow railwaymen.

By 5 January 1919 the circle had shown itself incapable of reaching a wider audience. On that day it dissolved itself and formed a new political organization, the *Deutsche Arbeiterpartei* (German Workers' Party). While still a tiny group, it did at least manage to acquire a total of forty-four members. Drexler became the leader of the new party. Its members were also able through their wider contacts within the Vril Society and the Thule Group to begin plotting actively against Soviet Bavaria.

At this stage of its existence the Vril Society's political obsessions predominated over its occult fantasies. Sebottendorf and his co-conspirators became involved in a succession of futile and inept attempts to overthrow the Marxist government.

Sebottendorf himself was primarily involved with the Thule Group, but the Vril Society was an inner circle within the organization that

Hitler reads through his Völkischer Beobachter *with obvious relish at his holiday home, the Berghof. Nazi triumphs were in evidence on practically every page.*

eventually merged with the larger group. Of the Vril Society's council of leaders none were more influential than Eckart and Karl Haushofer.

In spite of the small number of members who belonged to the Vril Society, its impact was out of all proportion to its size. It played a decisive part in the ascent of Hitler and the Nazis to supreme power within Germany.

THE SOCIETY OF THE GREEN DRAGON

The Vril Society originally derived from a Japanese group known as the Society of the Green Dragon, itself an offshoot of a Tibetan order. There were exactly seventy-two members of the Green Dragon and the aim of the society was said to be fomenting wars, revolutions and general destruction. Its origins are disputed, with some sources suggesting it was first formed by the ninth-century Japanese Buddhist mystic Kukai. He became enlightened by the Green Dragon Temple in Xian and his training consisted of occult and sexual magic traditions that first originated in Tibet. Another theory is that it was originally a Taoist order formed in China during the seventeenth century practising 'Taoist alchemy and immortalist techniques'. Other sources suggest that the society originated in Tibet where a green dragon symbolizes 'the God of thunder, bravery and all-conquering force'. It is known that the Japanese monk Ekai Kawaguchi visited Tibet twice before the First World War and at the very time that Haushofer was in Tokyo. Yet another suggestion is that it was an offshoot of the Black Dragon Society which first surfaced in 1901 and took its name from the Black Dragon River – better known as the River Amur – that separated Manchuria from Siberia. The Green Dragon River – the Qinglong – separates Manchuria and China. It has been suggested that the Green Dragon Society arose out of the Black Dragon organization.

The main objective of the members of the Green Dragon Society, to which Haushofer belonged, is said to have been to control the vital forces within the human body and become lords of time. Through the use of thought energy they believed that they possessed the power to fully activate all the chakras within both the physical and the astral body of humans. They also declared that the earth itself had an astral body and that both human and cosmic evolution were governed by the vital centres of the earth, which operated in a similar way to the chakras in the human body. The fall of Atlantis and the rise of the Aryan race were key moments in the history of the planet and the twentieth century was destined to see a similarly decisive new civilization emerging.

TIBETAN INFLUENCES ON THE VRIL SOCIETY

There were four main schools of religion within Tibet at the time Haushofer discovered its secret teachings. The most orthodox were the Gelug-pas, the Yellow Caps, whose head was the Dalai

Lama. Another school, the Kargyuptas, 'followers of the Apostolic Succession', believed in an unbroken line of gurus transmitting divine grace. There was also the Adi-Yoga school known as the Red Caps or the Unreformed Church. They were connected with the Yellow Caps but were regarded as having superior knowledge and powers in the area of occultism. Finally there were the Bons, known as the Black Caps, who believed in the pre-Buddhist animist religions and were considered powerful magicians.

The Kargyuptas did not believe in God but only in 'the law of cause and effect'. Their nearest approach to the idea of God was the concept of the Adi-Buddha which was said by them to be the 'life principle' and was identified with a more highly evolved type of human being. During their initiation ceremonies the teacher transmitted a form of this life principle which the disciple 'draws off', becoming 'endowed with power' as a result.

Many comparative religionists have been struck by the similarities between some of the teachings of the Kargyuptas and Gnosticism. The Gnostics were an early Christian group of heretics who believed that the material world was evil and had been created by Satan, whom they identified with the God of the Old Testament. Although the Kargyuptas no more believed in Satan than they did in God, they shared with Gnosticism the idea that the world was a state of being from which humans should attempt to escape and that knowledge, by which they meant spiritual enlightenment, was the path through which the world of matter could be overcome. The Gnostics, like the Kargyuptas, believed that this would lead to the emergence of a more highly evolved type of human who would be a semi-divine being. All of these ideas appealed not only to Haushofer but also to Eckart, Rosenberg, Hess, Himmler and Hitler. It was one reason why their own racist ideas went far beyond the simple prejudices of their times and took on a metaphysical dimension. Biology was destiny in their eyes and the task of raising the Aryan race to the next level of human evolution was seen as an urgent necessity.

Haushofer was a member of both the Japanese and the Tibetan societies and in 1919 he decided to found a German branch. He set up the society in Munich, originally calling it the Brothers of the Light. It was also known as the Luminous Lodge but before long its name was changed to the Vril Society.

LORD LYTTON AND THE ORIGINS OF VRIL

The name 'vril' came from a novel written in 1871 by the English writer Lord Lytton. In addition to being a popular novelist, Lytton was also a Freemason, a Rosicrucian and a dabbler in magic and the occult. Lytton's novel *The Coming Race* was set in a world where an advanced species lived beneath the earth in large caverns. They had developed the use of an energy form called *vril* which enabled them to be not just simply human but equal to the gods themselves. One day, Lytton told his readers, they would emerge from the bowels of the earth and rule the planet.

His novel paints a disturbing picture of a totalitarian and racist society. He wrote about his subterranean dwellers:

> *I arrived at the conclusion that this people – though originally not only of our human race but descended from the same ancestors as the great Aryan family – had yet now developed into a distinct species with which it was impossible that any community in the upper world could amalgamate. And that if they ever emerged from those nether recesses into the light of day, they would destroy and overcome our existent varieties of man.*

Lytton's novel ends with the gloomy conclusion, 'I pray that ages yet elapse before there emerges into sunlight our inevitable destroyers.'

In spite of his neglect nowadays, in his time Lytton was not only a highly popular novelist but was deeply involved in the occult. He exercised enormous influence upon the founders of the modern occult and magical revival begun by Eliphas Levi in France, the Theosophical

Society, the Golden Dawn and of course Haushofer, one of Hitler's principal mentors.

Lytton's novel proved particularly influential among German occult groups. The Vril Society was named in honour of his book and its members believed that the semi-divine beings that lived under the earth could make contact with humans and emerge on to the surface of the planet through various 'openings'. These 'underground Masters' as the Society referred to them possessed higher levels of knowledge and wisdom than ordinary humans. Some members of the Vril Society believed that they had established contact with these Masters and had acquired knowledge that could be used by them to dominate the human world. Eckart and Haushofer wanted to use *vril* power for political ends.

HAUSHOFER FOUNDS THE VRIL SOCIETY

The Society believed that the basis of all power was *vril*, the mysterious life force from which everything else emanated. Those who learned to master and control *vril* power would become Lords of the Earth. *Vril* is essentially the same as the energy referred to by Hindus as 'prana', by the Chinese and Japanese as 'chi' and by the early hypnotists as 'animal magnetism'.

In December 1919 the Vril Society met at a house near Berchtesgaden. A Croatian medium named Maria Orsitsch and another known simply as Sigrun transmitted a series of messages allegedly from the 'Secret Chiefs'. It was at this particular séance that the announcement was made of the imminent arrival of the longed-for saviour of Germany. The medium declared that he was 'hard by the door' and that he would be the next owner of the Spear of Destiny, part of the Imperial Regalia of Austria currently housed in the Hofburg Museum in Vienna.

In addition to holding séances to try and predict the future the Society also engaged in rituals to 'summon' and 'control' the *vril* power. Meditation and visualization exercises were practised for hours at a time in an attempt to develop and master the *vril* energy.

In The Coming Race, *Lord Lytton wrote about a superior subterranean master race and an energy form called* vril. *This brought him to the attention of the theosophists.*

HITLER JOINS THE VRIL SOCIETY

Not long afterwards Eckart invited Hitler to join the Vril Society. Under its influence he began to change into a confident, powerful speaker and develop the charisma that won him so many followers. The thirty-year-old Hitler seized on the opportunity to develop his 'willpower' and direct the force of his personality outwards in an attempt to influence events. Eckart became a close friend and mentor, as did Rosenberg. Later members of the Society included Hess, Goering and Himmler.

Hitler learned that the underground dwellers shared a common ancestry with the Aryan race and that the 'vril-ya' (as Lytton named his subterranean people) considered themselves superior to all other races. The vril-ya not only believed that the strong should rule over the weak and only the fittest should survive while the less fit should be crushed but they also believed in the unqualified right of their own branch of the Aryan race to dominate the world. Democracy, freedom and compassion were despised among the vril-ya, whose leader enjoyed absolute power and authority. The final goal of this ruler who employed vril power to control all natural and human activity was 'to attain to the purity of our species and supplant all the inferior races now existing'. In this single sentence of Lytton's book can be traced the subsequent development of Nazi racism and the seeds of genocide.

As well as their obsession with mastering vril power the Society's members also conducted extensive research into the legend of Atlantis. They became convinced that the lost continent was a northern land, in the vicinity of the Arctic, and that survivors from its destruction were the distant ancestors of the 'Nordic race'.

AGHARTI AND SHAMBALLAH

It was not only Atlantis but also the subterranean worlds of Agharti and Shamballah that interested the Vril Society. The land of Shamballah dates back to the seventeenth century, when it was first mentioned by a Jesuit missionary. He heard the story from Tibetan monks who claimed that the entrance to Shamballah lay in Mongolia. Apparently Shamballah, like the 'World Tree' of Norse and Teutonic mythology, was a place with both a world on the surface of the earth and a subterranean kingdom underneath.

The underground world of Shamballah was known as Agharti. Perhaps because of the powerful influence of Lytton's *The Coming Race* on a whole generation of occult thinkers, Haushofer, along with some Russian exiles of a mystical inclination, came to see Agharti as the dwelling place of the Secret Chiefs.

Haushofer claimed that he first heard of Agharti and Shamballah in 1905 while he was in Central Asia. It was a vast underground realm beneath the Himalayas inhabited by a race of superior beings. The kingdom itself was known as Agharti and Shamballah was its capital.

Haushofer described Agharti as 'a place of meditation, a hidden city of goodness, a temple of non-participation in the things of the world'. By contrast Shamballah was 'a city of violence and power whose forces command the elements and the masses of humanity, and hasten the arrival of the human race at the turning point of time'.

Haushofer claimed that his initiators had revealed to him that after the fall of Atlantis many survivors had travelled through Europe and Asia before eventually settling in large underground caves beneath the mountains in Tibet. He declared that cave dwelling adepts still flourished and continued to direct the course of world civilization from their underground sanctuaries. Haushofer did not believe that the underground world of Agharti lay in Mongolia and insisted upon its Tibetan location. His influence upon Hitler led to a number of expeditions to Tibet by the Nazis from 1926 to 1942. The most important of these visits took place in 1938.

Shamballah's full title was Chang Shambhala, a name that means 'northern quietness'. It has a connotation similar to the word Hyperborean which means 'at the back of the north wind'. Shamballah plays a considerable part in Tibetan tradition but it is overwhelmingly located outside Tibet, in Mongolia or Siberia. Here the role played by the Bons in preserving many traditional beliefs and practices from outside the country almost certainly accounts for the entry of a legend that originated elsewhere in the Tibetan mythos.

It was through the Bons, combining Buddhist teachings with older traditions, that the Kalachakra school of Lamaism came into Tibet. The name of the system means the Wheel of Time and it looks to the sky above with a sun around which seven planets circle. Kala,

In Buddhist thought, Shamballah (seen above) is a fabulous kingdom whose reality is as visionary or spiritual as it is grounded in any geographical reality. Early proto-Nazis seem to have been attracted to a variety of myths, which they then used as the basis for their ideology.

which means 'time', drives a chariot with seven wheels and controls it through the use of seven reins. The Tibetans stress that the origin of this school of Lamaism lay outside the country, generally suggesting Mongolia.

Shamballah was described by almost every writer as an earthly but hidden paradise. It has been called 'the holy place where the earthly world links with the highest states of consciousness'. It extends upwards into the sky and downwards into a subterranean kingdom. This part of the Shamballah legend definitely originated in Mongolia and the underground world was known as Agharti or Agartha, a word meaning 'inaccessible'. The ruler of Agharti was often referred to as the King of the World and was said to be able to exert telepathic influence over people on the surface of the earth.

At some stage the King of the World and the people of Agharti would emerge and conquer the world. Shamballah and Agharti would become the fountainhead of power. It was said that:

> the prophecy that the King of Shamballah, who is sometimes called the Chief of the Secret Tibetan Brotherhood of Initiates of the Occult Sciences, shall govern mankind, implies the coming of a golden age and the enthronement of Divine Wisdom on earth.

THE RUSSIAN CHARLATAN BADMAEV

Another possible connection between Agharti and Haushofer is the Russian charlatan Badmaev. His career has been described as follows:

> One of the most curious phenomena of the Russian Imperial Court was the 'doctor of Tibetan medicine', Badmaev. Shamzaran Badmaev affirmed that he has acquired an exact knowledge of the secret doctrines of 'Tibetan magic' and medical science in his father's house (Transbaikalia), as the knowledge was an ancient tradition in the family. In the course of time medicine and politics and 'lotus essences' became more and more involved in each other, resulting in a fantastic

political sorcery that had its origin in the Badmaev sanatorium and that decided the destiny of Russia.

Badmaev appears to have been a Buryat Siberian but he certainly visited Tibet and learned the language. He translated the Tibetan medical treatise *Zhud-shi* into Russian. Badmaev also developed a number of herbal remedies.

In the 1860s Badmaev converted to Christianity and was baptized into the Russian Orthodox Church. He explained his decision as follows:

> *I was the Lama-Buddhist, deeply believing and convinced, knew Shamanism and Shamans, beliefs of my ancestors. I have left the Buddhism, without despising and without humiliating their insights but only because the doctrine of Christ the Saviour has got into my feelings with such clearness that this doctrine of Christ the Saviour has lit up all my being.*

Badmaev changed his name from Tsultim to Peter but continued to practise his Tibetan medicine. He also revisited China, Mongolia and Tibet where he met with members of the Bons, Lamas, Kargyuptas and Red Caps. His medical treatments included powders and grasses. Badmaev certainly set out to create myths about his life and he was alleged not only to have been 113 years old when he died but to have fathered a daughter at the age of 100!

The crucial fact about Badmaev is the clear connection between Russian Shamanism and magical traditions and practices from Mongolia and Tibet. He was certainly familiar with the stories of Agharti and Shamballah and it is inconceivable that a man as well known as him would not have attracted the interest of Haushofer.

MONGOLIAN INITIATES

Another source for the Nazi preoccupation with Agharti was through Russian émigrés. Roman von Ungern-Sternberg came originally from

Estonia and claimed to be descended from the Teutonic Knights. Following the Russian Revolution he joined up with Admiral Kolchak's anti-Bolshevik armies and fought in Siberia. His troops held out against the Red Army until 1920, when he retreated into Mongolia. He converted to Buddhism and announced that he was a reincarnation of Genghis Khan and would lead the Mongols to a similar destiny of world conquest.

After fighting three battles with the Mongolian dictator he captured the capital and made himself ruler of the country. Ungern-Sternberg promptly installed electricity and radio in the city and declared himself to be 'the God of War'. He proclaimed that he was the precursor of the coming King of the World and was allied to the secret leaders of Agharti. Ungern-Sternberg promised to found a Greater Mongolia stretching as far north as Lake Baikal as well as restoring the monarchy in Russia and China. He was a fanatical anti-Semite who claimed that all Communists were Jews. As soon as he captured the Mongolian capital he ordered a pogrom against what must have been a very small Jewish population.

After nine months as ruler of the country he led a band of Mongol warriors into Siberia. Following several battles with Communist forces he was defeated, captured and executed.

MEN, BEASTS AND GODS

It was the publication of a highly colourful book in 1923 that not only brought Ungern-Sternberg's name into prominence but also introduced the idea of Agharti to a wider audience. *Men, Beasts and Gods* became a best-seller and once more stimulated German interest in Tibet, Mongolia and the Far East.

Ferdinand Ossendowski was a natural storyteller and his book *Men, Beasts and Gods* is a mixture of fact, sensationalism, speculation and downright invention. In spite of his claims it is certain that Ossendowski never went to Tibet. On the other hand he was in Mongolia and did meet with Ungern-Sternberg and a number of other larger-than-life characters, some of whom were Tibetan. In Mongolia he also met a Siberian by the name of Tushegoun Lama. Tushegoun claimed to be a personal friend of the Dalai Lama and told Ossendowski many things about Tibet. He also made an intriguing reference to the 'King of the World in Agharti', claiming that he was the only living man who 'was ever in Agharti', a revelation that fascinated and intrigued Ossendowski.

Later he met other Tibetan exiles in Mongolia who gave him more details than the reticent Siberian informant. One of them told him 'the subterranean people have reached the highest knowledge. Now it is a large kingdom, millions of men, with the "King of the World" as their ruler'. The other man told Ossendowski that 'the kingdom is called Agharti. It extends throughout the subterranean passage of the whole world'. Later still another Tibetan exile in Mongolia told him that the gypsies had lived in Agharti for many centuries and when they emerged they brought with them the psychic powers they had learned from the Secret Chiefs of the underground kingdom.

Ossendowski met Ungern-Sternberg and became fascinated by his vision. He also met the Tashi Lama who was exiled to Mongolia following a feud with the Dalai Lama. The Tashi Lama claimed that in his old monastery of Shigatse there was a message from the King of the World written on tablets of gold. No one had been able to decipher the writing on them which was in an unknown language but in a state of enlightenment the meaning of the tablets 'penetrated the Lama's brain'. The Tashi Lama claimed that he had been King of Shamballah in a previous incarnation. During his exile he founded many Kalachakra schools in Mongolia and north-west China. The Tashi claimed to be in direct touch with the Masters of Shamballah.

Ossendowski's account seems highly fanciful and even on the publication of his book it was denounced by the Swedish explorer Sven Hedin as a fabrication. There is certainly no doubt that Ossendowski's claim to have visited Tibet is false as Hedin, who had made several previous expeditions to that country, demonstrated clearly. He also pointed out that the story of Agharti was probably lifted wholesale from a nineteenth-century French writer.

On the other hand, the story of Agharti predates the source Hedin gives by at least twenty years. It was also claimed by the author cited by the Swedish explorer that he had heard of 'Agartha' (as he called it) from an Indian adept. In addition the Mongolian part of Ossendowski's adventures rings true. In particular his account of Ungern-Sternberg's attitudes and behaviour is corroborated from independent sources including a distant relative, Count Hermann Keyserling. The accounts he gives of Shamballah and Agharti are also supported by other Mongolian sources.

There is little doubt that Ossendowski was a romancer who frequently 'improved' upon the stories he was told, a plagiarist of other writers' work and one who invented some of his material out of whole cloth, but the probability remains that the core of his book is true. Agharti may or may not be an account of an actual place past or present but there is no doubt that, perhaps because of its assimilability with Lytton's fictional race of *vril-ya*, the myth attracted considerable support within the Vril Society.

NAZI ATTITUDE TO FACTS

Many Nazis, including Hitler, had a curious attitude towards facts. When for instance he was told bluntly by Rauschning that the *Protocols of the Learned Elders of Zion* was a crude forgery, Hitler's response was strange. He did not dispute Rauschning's statement but simply replied that he did not care. What Hitler found 'appalling' about them was what he described as their 'intrinsic truth'.

In the same way Haushofer and other initiates of the Vril Society were not concerned with the absolute veracity of the Agharti story. What concerned them was its 'intrinsic truth', which in their eyes meant the genuine existence upon the planet of a superior race of subterranean beings. Legends of underground dwellers are very ancient and can be found in stories dating back at least as far as 3000BC. The general tendency nowadays is to regard them as mythical or symbolic but the Vril Society took them literally, as many religious believers have for thousands of years.

NAZI EXPEDITIONS TO TIBET

Haushofer's conviction that Agharti and Shamballah lay in Tibet rather than Mongolia led to a number of Nazi expeditions in search of these fabled lands. As well as exploring Tibet, they also recruited teams of 'spelunkers' to descend into caves and mines in Germany, Italy and Switzerland. They were directed by the *Ahnenerbe* to seek out tunnels and other possible entrances to the 'subterranean kingdom' of the *vril-ya*. A German army colonel was even ordered to research Lytton's life to try and discover the location of the caves he had mentioned in his novel.

UNDERGROUND TUNNELS IN CZECHOSLOVAKIA

In 1939 two German expeditions were sent to Czechoslovakia to investigate tunnels and mines that might be linked to an underground world. One of the sites on which they worked was later found by a Czech resistance group in October 1944. The group's leader, Dr Antonin Horak, described how the partisans came across a tunnel while sheltering in a large underground cavern. Horak explored the tunnel for some distance before he came across a section that appeared to be recent and was clearly man-made.

> Lighting some torches I saw that I was in a spacious, curved, black shaft formed by cliff-like walls. The floor in the incline was a solid lime pavement.

It was clear that the tunnel extended far beyond the area that he could see by the light of his flickering torches. Attempting to extract samples of material he discovered not only that his pickaxe failed to loosen the lime pavement but that even firing his pistol at the wall had no effect.

The frustrated Horak had to abandon the attempt to obtain samples. He wrote:

I sat there by the fire speculating. How far did it reach into the rocks, I wondered. Who, or what, put it into the mountain? Was it man-made? And was it at last proof of the truth in legends – like Plato's – of long lost civilizations with magic technologies which our reason cannot grasp or believe?

Whatever secrets the tunnel within the cave may have held remain a mystery to this day. All that Horak could do was abandon his attempt and then some years later give an account of his strange discovery.

ERNST SCHÄFER'S EXPEDITION TO TIBET

Ernst Schäfer took part in three expeditions to Tibet, one in 1931–2, another in 1934–6 and his most important one in 1938–9. Schäfer led this last expedition under the sponsorship of the *Ahnenerbe* at a time when the Nazis were seeking to recruit Asian allies in the event of war. He published an account of his journey in a 1950 book, *In Fest der Weissen Schieler: eine Forscherfahrt durch Tibet nach Lhasa der heiligen Stadt des Gottkönigtums* (Festival of the White Scarves: a research journey through Tibet to Lhasa, the holy city of the God Kings).

Schäfer's reception in Tibet was a mixed one. The powerful Nechung oracle issued a warning that Germany's leader was 'like a dragon'. Tibet was in a difficult position with pro-Chinese, pro-Japanese and pro-British parties within the government and its principal consideration was to avoid becoming involved in any sort of military conflict.

The outbreak of war made full-scale expeditions such as Schäfer's impractical. A further visit to Tibet is said to have occurred in 1942–3 but the details are so sketchy that it is impossible to form any conclusions upon the matter. The Nazi desire to discover and harness *vril* power remained no more than a dream.

The Ernst Schäfer Expedition to Tibet at Gangtok, 1938: Ernst Schäfer is fourth from the left and the expedition was sponsored by Heinrich Himmler and the SS.

WHAT IS *VRIL* POWER?

What exactly is this mysterious *vril* over which the Nazis expended so much time, effort and money? Lytton, in his novel, remarks:

> *There is no word in any language I know that is an exact synonym for vril. I should call it electricity, except that it comprehends in its manifold branches other forces of nature, to which, in our scientific nomenclature, different names are assigned, such as magnetism, galvanism, etc. These people consider that in vril they have arrived at the unity in natural energic agencies, which has been conjectured by many philosophers above ground, and which Faraday thus intimated under the misleading term of correlation.*
>
> *These subterranean philosophers assert that, by one operation of vril, which Faraday would perhaps call 'atmospheric magnetism',*

they can influence the variations of temperature – in plain words, the weather; that by other operations, akin to those ascribed to mesmerism, electrobiology, odic force, etc, but applied scientifically through vril *conductors, they can exercise influence over minds, and bodies animal and vegetable, to an extent unsurpassed in the romance of our mystics. To all such agencies they give the common name of* vril.

Lytton was writing a work of fiction but did admit to a friend that he believed *vril* power really existed though he gave no reason for his belief. Others were less reticent or hesitant and identified *vril* with all kinds of other forms of energy.

The Vril Society believed that *vril* was a force which if controlled could be used as a means of acquiring spiritual enlightenment, to heal people or to dominate the wills of others. They also believed that *vril* could be used to influence events on the material plane by concentrating the willpower while it was focused into a kind of laser beam through a combination of visualization and directed emotion. The final link in the chain was establishing a means of communicating with the Secret Chiefs and harnessing their powers.

THE SOCIETY'S METHODS OF RAISING *VRIL* POWER

The Society employed two methods that it believed would enable the initiate to control and manipulate *vril* power. The first was known as the 'scientific way' and involved chemically isolating particles of a proton found within lead after which they had to be 'captured' in 'the photonic magnetism of Saturn' or placed in lava from an active volcano. A chemical process was then alleged to follow that would make the initiate a master of *vril* power.

The alternative method was known as the 'mystic way' and involved the initiate standing before a symbol representing Agharti with coloured lights and sonic vibrations in the background. It was then supposed to 'effect a symbolic regression of life' after which he would be filled with *vril* power.

Hitler had no scientific background at all and would certainly have been trained in the 'mystic way'. How effective all these rituals actually were is open to question but there is no doubt that Hitler's personality and ability to influence other people developed enormously as a result of his training in the Vril Society.

As the Nazi Party grew and Hitler became a full-time politician his direct involvement with the Society decreased and became sporadic. In spite of that the mere presence in his inner circle of men like Rosenberg, Hess and Himmler mean that the ethos of *vril* was constantly in the background.

ROCKET SCIENTIST WILLY LEY REVEALS THE SECRETS OF THE VRIL SOCIETY

The very existence of the Vril Society remained a secret until the end of the Second World War. At the Nuremberg Trials some defendants mentioned Agharti and Shamballah but their testimony was dismissed or ignored, largely because the prosecution wanted to avoid insanity pleas. It was the German rocket scientist Willy Ley who first introduced the world to the Vril Society. In a 1947 essay entitled 'Pseudo-sciences under the Nazi regime' he explained that the Society was founded on the belief that Lytton's subterranean world was literally true and that *vril* power could help to create an Aryan super race. Tibetans were also invited to join the Society because of Haushofer's belief that Agharti lay within their country.

The Society's members believed that they had acquired knowledge of *vril* power and could become as powerful as the underground dwellers. Ley revealed that they had developed 'a whole system of internal gymnastics' by which the control of *vril* power could be achieved. He described how the Society invited members from across the world to assist them in researching and developing Aryan supermen.

These included a number of Tibetan Lamas with knowledge of Agharti. These monks lived in Berlin and worked with Haushofer and the *Ahnenerbe*. Their leader was known as 'the Man with Green Gloves' and he made a number of successful predictions about Hitler and the Nazis. In 1945, as Soviet troops entered Berlin, they were astonished to discover a number of Tibetan corpses dressed in German uniform but bearing no badges or insignia of rank. The bodies lay on the ground in orderly ranks, a ritual knife beside them which they had used to commit suicide by piercing their stomachs rather than face the indignity of capture. It was a tragic end for the dark initiates of Agharti.

Such was the mental atmosphere in which Hitler moved between 1919 and 1923. To some extent the effects of his training lasted for the rest of his life. Certainly he remained convinced of the ability of willpower to manipulate events until the bitter end.

Small in number, full of bizarre and unscientific notions, the Vril Society nevertheless wielded a power and influence out of all proportion to the size of its membership. The millions squandered on

Himmler envisaged Wewelsburg Castle as the Nazi Camelot, centrepiece of a Reich that would last a thousand years. In the event, the Nazis only held power for twelve years and Wewelsburg proved a costly folly.

Wewelsburg Castle and a vast number of pseudo-scientific and occult 'projects', and the poisonous racial fantasies that ended in genocide, all had their origins in the rituals and doctrines that Hitler imbibed from the Vril Society.

Chapter Three
A NEW RELIGION FOR GERMANY

AT THE HEART of the Nazi appeal to the nation was its conscious attempt to present itself as a new religion. In this creed Hitler was openly hailed as the saviour of Germany, *Mein Kampf* was accorded equal status with the Bible as a 'holy book' and numerous activities were devised to celebrate the Party, the nation and its leader. These were all consciously modelled on Christian ceremonies and traditions.

NAZI HOSTILITY TO CHRISTIANITY

Many Nazis were fiercely anti-Christian but in public at least Hitler adopted a moderate and placatory tone, particularly towards Catholicism. In private his views were every bit as extreme and hostile towards Christianity as those of Rosenberg, Himmler and Hess. Rauschning summarized a conversation in which the *Führer* had remarked:

> *When the time came, Hitler would bring the world a new religion. The blessed consciousness of eternal life in union with the great universal life, and in membership of an immortal people – that was the message he would impart to the world when the time came. Hitler would be the first to achieve what Christianity was meant to have been, a joyous message that liberated men from the things that burdened their life. Hitler would restore men to the self-confident divinity with which nature had endowed them.*

NAZISM AS A SUBSTITUTE RELIGION

National Socialism specifically set out to activate the religious impulse within the German people and to transfer that sentiment to the Party and above all to its leader. Hitler was presented as the proper focus of worship, his ideals as the true religion of the nation and his party as the true Church to which all true Germans should belong. Every attempt was made to give the people a substitute religion with ceremonies, dogmas and objects of worship. Of course the degree to which such things were pushed varied, with Hitler always being far more cautious in public than his lieutenants, but the general drift of Nazism was clear and the effect of this constant attempt to supplant Christianity with its own ideas was pervasive.

> *In Mein Kampf Hitler spoke of the need for an inward religious longing at the moment when out of the purely metaphysical/ unbounded world of ideas a clearly bounded faith forms itself.*

With near-religious fervour, a torchlit procession in honour of the newly elected Chancellor, Adolf Hitler, passes along Wilhelmstrasse, Berlin on 30 January 1933.

Assuredly, this faith is not an end in itself, but only a means to an end; yet it is the indispensable necessary means which alone makes it possible to attain the end. The highest ideals always correspond to the deepest vital necessity. In helping to raise man from the level of mere animal survival, faith really contributes to the securing and safeguarding of man's existence. Take away from present mankind our religious-dogmatic principles which are upheld by its education and whose practical significance is that of ethical-moral principles, by abolishing religious education and without replacing it by something equivalent and the result facing you will be a grave shock to the foundations of mankind's existence. One may therefore state that not only does man live to serve higher ideals but that, conversely, these higher ideals also provide the presupposition of his existence as man. So the circle closes.

In spite of the characteristically turgid prose the meaning of Hitler's words is clear. National Socialism's dogmas and ceremonies were designed to replace religion just as the Party itself was to be the substitute for the role of churches.

In his *Table Talk* Hitler announced his intention to destroy all religious bodies once he had won the war. He declared that he had become convinced of 'the fallacy of all religions' and that only the survival of the race mattered.

For most of its existence the Weimar Republic grappled with huge practical problems and on the whole failed to solve them. Its leaders were for the most part well-meaning intellectuals who were out of their depth with the successive crises that gripped their country and above all had neither the ability nor the desire to reach out to the ordinary Germans and offer them a positive vision. That is why the broad mass of the citizens turned away from the democratic parties in despair and voted instead for a party promising them national salvation.

HITLER AS THE SAVIOUR OF GERMANY

Just as he tried to make the Nazi Party replace the churches so too Hitler consciously set out to present himself as the new Messiah for Germany. He demanded of his followers the characteristically religious qualities of obedience, self-sacrifice and faith. On the very evening of Hitler's appointment as Chancellor, Goebbels organized a huge triumphal parade in Berlin. Thousands of Nazi supporters donned their uniforms and marched to the Chancellery to pay tribute to Hitler. Massed bands played martial music to accompany the torchlit procession of SA (*Sturmabteilung*) and SS members welcoming the triumph of their leader to the background of a live radio broadcast on the event.

The constant and relentless barrage of propaganda under the regime reiterated the idea of Hitler as the saviour of the German nation and as the leader chosen for the country by God. In a very real sense Hitler was elevated to the same status as Christ and it became increasingly common for him to be seen as a semi-divine being rather than simply a politician. Nothing like it had been seen since the time of the Divine Right of Kings and even the personality cult of Stalin was not quite on the same level of exaltation.

NAZISM AS RELIGIOUS RITUAL

Throughout his political career Hitler conducted his public meetings in the form of rituals, almost of church services. He always spoke in the evening and declared that only then could the appropriate atmosphere of expectation be properly created. Hitler always began his speeches by giving a history of the Party followed by some policy announcements and then a violent denunciation of Germany's enemies. He concluded by announcing his absolute resolve to stand firm and maintain and extend the nation's greatness.

The enemies he singled out for blame most often were of course the Jews. To an extent the very act of praising or blaming has religious overtones and to his audiences and readers Hitler's constant insistence

Hitler speaks to massive crowds in the Lustgarten, Berlin, in his self-appointed role of 'new Messiah'.

that he stood for goodness and positive values while the Jews represented evil and negativity seemed an entirely acceptable denunciation of sin. As Hitler put it in *Mein Kampf* in an extraordinary passage (even by the standards of that book)

> *I believe I am acting according to the intention of the Almighty Creator: by resisting the Jews I am doing the work of the Lord!*

Hardly any of the Nazi leaders believed in Christianity. Hitler privately claimed to be an atheist in spite of the many muddled occult beliefs he held. Goebbels and Goering also expressed similar views, with in all three cases the ideas of 'Blood and Soil' and the Aryan race forming the nearest thing in their world view to any kind of genuinely religious sentiments. Rosenberg and Robert Ley (head of the Labour Front) subscribed to an essentially Gnostic view of the world and both Himmler and Baldur von Schirach (leader of the Hitler Youth) were outspoken advocates of a revived paganism.

THE CONCORDAT WITH THE VATICAN

Although Hitler had been raised as a Catholic his decision on 3 July 1933 to sign a treaty with the Vatican was an action motivated entirely by *realpolitik* rather than any kind of vestigial Catholicism. There were three main reasons why he chose to come to an arrangement with the Church rather than fight it openly. The first was a desire to persuade the Catholic Centre Party to vote itself out of existence in return for a concordat with the Vatican; and two days after the agreement was signed the Centre Party did dissolve itself. The second reason was a direct complaint by Paul von Hindenburg to Hitler about the aggressively anti-Christian rhetoric of some Nazi leaders. Hindenburg remained President for the first eighteen months of Hitler's Chancellorship and was deeply concerned about the confrontational nature of the relationship between the government and the churches.

Jackbooted members of the SA fix a sign to a shop window warning passers-by not to shop at Jewish businesses like this one, 1933.

Many of his Cabinet, including the Vice-Chancellor, Papen, were Catholics and they found the anti-religious bias of the Nazis distasteful. With the situation in the country still tense, Hindenburg asked Hitler to tone down his campaign and reluctantly he agreed. The third and perhaps most important reason was to neutralize the power of the Church over German Catholics and make them more willing to co-operate with the regime.

RELIGIOUS DIVISIONS IN GERMANY

Germany had suffered from religious division for hundreds of years. During the Middle Ages it had produced more heretics than any other European country with the possible exception of France. Germany was particularly prone to explosions of apocalyptic and Messianic movements and when the Reformation polarized Europe between Protestantism and Catholicism the country was split down the middle. During the horrific Thirty Years War (1618–48), Germany was devastated as France, Spain, Austria, Sweden, Denmark and various bands of mercenaries ravaged the country in the name of religion. When Germany was finally united under Bismarck it was essentially as a result of a war of conquest, which saw Protestant Prussia defeat Catholic Austria and exclude it from the new Germany. Catholic kingdoms like Bavaria were forcibly incorporated into the new Protestant Reich. When Bismarck instituted his *Kulturkampf* (cultural struggle) against Catholicism the Pope mobilized German Catholics to resist and the result was the birth of the Centre Party which tried to defend Catholic interests on the political level.

The religious divisions within Germany never really healed and all forms of Christianity began to decline as a growing tendency to disbelieve in traditional religion spread. German theologians had been among the leading figures in the attempt to create a rationalist version of Christianity but their efforts tended to destroy rather than renew religious faith. Ironically their work helped to fuel a growing anti-Semitism within Germany by virtually abandoning the Old Testament and thus implicitly separating Christianity from its Jewish origins.

PAGAN REVIVALISM AND VÖLKISCH CHRISTIANITY

In addition, not only did romantic neo-pagan movements begin to revive with men like Wagner and Guido von List as their most prominent exponents but a growing tendency to create a *völkisch* Christianity began to develop. The anti-Semitism of this new trend varied but became more pronounced from the 1890s onwards. Leading exponents of *völkisch* Christianity were Julius Langbehn, Paul de Lagarde and Ernst von Bunsen. The trend among *völkisch* Christians became one of denying any connection between Christianity and Judaism. The absurd suggestion by the philosopher Fichte that Jesus was not even Jewish but actually an Aryan was enthusiastically adopted by this school of thought. Bunsen declared that the Bible's real religion was one of Aryan sun worship. Adam of course was an Aryan and the Serpent in the Garden of Eden was a Jew. Wagner described the

Jews as 'the devil incarnate of human decadence' and called for 'a Final Solution' to 'the Jewish problem'.

Lagarde was a fanatical racist who described the Slavs as 'the burden of history', as 'material for use in constructing new German formations', and expressed the opinion that 'the sooner they perish the better it will be for us and for them'. He saw Jesus as a man unfortunate enough to be born among the Jews by accident and whose greatness consisted in the alleged desire of 'not wanting to be a Jew'. Lagarde described German Protestants as carrying on 'the rotten remains of Christianity' and the Catholic Church as 'the born enemy of all States and nations'. He called for the immediate abolition of all synagogues.

Lagarde called for a new 'German faith' which would be instituted by a man with 'a pure and strong will'. In his book *The Religion of the Future* he wrote:

> We want liberty, not liberalism; Germany, not Judaeo-Celtic theories about Germany; piety, not dogmatics; we want our own nature to be acknowledged, educated and transfigured; we do not want to be driven by a Russian coachman holding French reins, or flogged by a Jewish whip.

He called for 'the destruction of Judaism' and declared that 'the Jews will cease to be Jews to the same extent that we become ourselves. Every Jew is a proof of the weakness of our national life and of the small worth of what we call the Christian religion'. Lagarde also proposed deporting the Jews of Europe to Madagascar. This idea was seriously considered by the Nazis for a while, who were undoubtedly under the influence of his philosophy.

THE BEGINNING OF THE GERMAN CHRISTIAN MOVEMENT

By 1917 three leading exponents of what became known by its advocates as 'German Christianity' put forward 95 theses in imitation of Luther's original 95 theses posted in 1517. The authors of the theses believed that religion should be based upon their new interpretation of Christianity. They denounced 'the Jewish religion' and wanted to remove the whole of the Old Testament from the Bible and most of the New Testament as well.

By 1921 the League for German Churches was founded and in its bi-monthly magazine it spoke of Jesus as 'a tragic Aryan figure'. It called for the Old Testament to be replaced with 'a German myth'.

With the growing success of the Nazi Party the League and similar groups began to come together to work with and support the Nazis. Many senior Nazis tried to influence the 'German Christians' to go in a more overtly racist and nationalist direction. Rosenberg was the prime mover in this attempted liaison.

The Nazis tried to use 'German Christianity' as a vehicle for Nazifying the churches, but ultimately their own beliefs were bitterly hostile to even such a pale shadow of Christianity. Hitler described the entire Christian religion as a 'Jewish swindle' and Himmler considered it 'utterly unGerman'. Attempts were made to set up a 'German Church' for Protestants where these views were literally preached into the minds of worshippers.

THE NAZI CRUSADE AGAINST THE CHURCHES

With Hindenburg's death in 1934 Hitler and his government were free to resume their attacks upon Christianity. There were genuine ideological reasons for their attitudes, most notably the fact that Christianity offered salvation to all believers while for the Nazis only the Aryan race could be saved. Himmler and Rosenberg also had their own strange religious ideas and were determined to impose them upon the German people. On the whole they were far more successful in the act of repression than they were in generating a significant degree of support for their views.

The most important single reason for the crusade against the churches was expressed by Martin Bormann in his Order of 6–7 June 1941 to the *Gauleiters*, which said:

All influences which might restrict or even damage the leadership of the people expressed by the Führer with the aid of the NSDAP [Nazi Party] must be eliminated. Never again must the churches be allowed any influence over the leadership of the people. This must be broken totally and forever. Only then will the existence of nation and Reich be assured.

Hitler left Rosenberg in charge of making the German churches fall into line with National Socialist philosophy. Rosenberg's confrontational approach made many enemies and even drew the condemnation of the Pope. Serious problems were created by the attempt to Nazify the churches and particularly the Protestant ones. The Catholics had been relatively critical while Pius XI was Pope but his successor Pius XII was far more accommodating to the Nazis. He was the man who as a cardinal had been largely responsible for signing the concordat between the Vatican and the Nazis. Even the Holocaust – of which he was well aware – did not stir him to condemn the regime. At no point did he attack the Nazis in public and it was left to a few brave individual Catholic clergymen to try and uphold Christian values in the face of a sustained campaign that often employed brutal violence and even murder when dealing with religious believers.

THE GERMAN EVANGELICAL CHURCH

The German Evangelical Church was headed by the pro-Nazi Bishop Ludwig Müller and was at first regarded as a means of unifying Protestants behind Hitler. It called for a 'people's church' with membership restricted to those of 'good German blood'. Müller was an army chaplain and his first action on becoming the leader of German Protestantism was to speak in militaristic terms of Christian soldiers fighting a crusade against the forces of evil. He also introduced the Horst Wessel chant 'banners up, close the ranks, free the streets for the Brown battalions' into church ritual. When he preached he wore his two Iron Crosses over his cassock and he employed cavalry trumpeters

Pope Pius XI (right) celebrates the 10th anniversary of his election at St Michael's Church in Berlin: he was no pushover when it came to the Nazis and their bullying.

to play military fanfares during his services. Müller and his supporters dismissed clergy with Jewish ancestors and even those who were married to 'non-Aryans'. They excluded from membership Jews who had converted to Christianity or whose ancestors had done so.

The 'German Christians' called for the Old Testament 'with its tales of cattle merchants and pimps' to be abandoned completely and regarded as an entirely non-Christian book. Even the New Testament in their eyes needed 'revision' to make Jesus' teachings 'conform entirely with the demands of National Socialism'. They demanded that all Church leaders should pledge full loyalty to Hitler and exclude converted Jews from their congregation. Their slogan became 'one people, one Reich, one faith'.

The Nazis intended or at least hoped that the majority of Protestants in Germany would become part of Müller's Church. That attempt was never successful and most German Protestants remained within the mainstream Lutheran Churches. The attack on the independence of the churches and the attempt to impose Nazi racial ideas upon them and make them an integral part of their doctrine actually roused fierce opposition.

ROSENBERG AND POSITIVE CHRISTIANITY

Rosenberg spoke glibly of what he called 'positive Christianity', which in essence meant a Christianity that was not only stripped of its Jewish heritage but which also denied the essential Christian values and replaced them instead with a mish-mash of racist and *völkisch* ideas. He was too much of a remote intellectual to understand that such a concept could never have succeeded in gaining the loyalty and allegiance of genuine Christians.

Rosenberg drew up a programme for a 'National Reich Church' during the early stages of the Second World War. His proposals were approved by Hitler and represented an attempt to suppress utterly the Christian religion in Germany. Had the war gone differently Christianity would have faced a level of persecution it had not experienced since the

The 'German Christians' were a Protestant group aligned with the Nazis and their ideology. The idea was to make individual Protestant churches into a single, pro-Hitler body.

time of the Roman Empire. It would have been replaced by Rosenberg's bizarre 'Thirty Articles' among which were:

5   The National Church is determined to exterminate irrevocably . . . the strange and foreign Christian faiths imported into Germany. . .

13   The National Church demands immediate cessation of the publishing and the dissemination of the Bible in Germany. . .

18   The National Church will clear away from its altars all crucifixes, Bibles and pictures of saints.

19   On the altars there must be nothing but *Mein Kampf* (to the German nation and therefore to God the most sacred book) and to the left of the altar a sword.

30   On the day of its foundation, the Christian Cross must be removed from all churches, cathedrals and chapels. . . and it

must be superseded by the only unconquerable symbol, the swastika.

THE GERMAN FAITH MOVEMENT

Far more moderate than Rosenberg, Himmler or even Müller, Wilhelm Hauer was a scholar and an expert on Indian culture, religion and history. In 1933 he published a book that became the 'foundation document' of the 'German Christians'. Anti-Semitism is not one of the principal platforms of Hauer's book and he stresses that Christianity is an irrelevant alien tradition rather than being directly opposed to 'Aryanism'. The work is full of comparisons between Norse myth, Hindu mythology, philosophers like Plato and Hegel, mystics like Jakob Boehme and Meister Eckhart and writers like Goethe, all thrown together in a scholarly but ultimately polemical manner for the 'freeing' of the German people from 'Jewish influence'.

For Hauer 'German culture' has its own 'gospels', the ancient Norse and Teutonic myths. Wotan is the true God of the Germans and not the Christian God. German virtues are justice, nobility and capacity for sacrifice as opposed to Christian ones like compassion. Hauer declared that the modern rejection of Christianity came from a new belief in 'the inviolability of the noble man's will' and he believed that it was 'the sole ground from which a genuine and adequate faith may arise'. In his eyes, the rebirth of a 'German faith' was imminent because Hitler and the Nazis had created a situation where it could become 'an historical reality'.

This bizarre but influential work attracted a highly favourable review from the psychologist Carl Jung, who announced that it 'cannot be read without profound emotion'. In Jung's eyes,

there are representatives of the German Faith Movement who, both intellectually and in human terms, are fully in a position not merely to believe but also to know that the God of the Germans is Wotan and not the universal God of the Christians.

HITLER STANDS APART FROM THE STRUGGLE

Hitler himself on the whole tried to stand apart from the struggle. Himmler and Rosenberg were the most vocally anti-Christian members of his Cabinet, but Hess declared that 'atheists' had 'modified' the teachings of Christianity; Goering spoke of 'finding a way back to the primeval voices of our race'; and von Schirach announced his intention to 'overcome' Christianity. Count Reventlow told a crowd of 15,000 people that the 'ancient deities' were still alive in the hearts of every German who was true to his or her 'blood and soil'. In 1938 carols and nativity plays were banned in schools and even the word Christmas was officially replaced by Yuletide.

CATHOLIC OPPOSITION TO THE NAZIS

From the very beginning of the Nazi campaign against the churches there was opposition. The Catholics refused to accept that Hitler possessed greater authority over them than the Pope and the head of Catholic Action was murdered by the Nazis. Following an agreement between the Vatican and Hitler the worst excesses were toned down.

Wotan heals Balder's wounded horse as three goddesses watch on. The Nazis took ancient Norse and Teutonic myths as true articles of German faith.

Individual Catholic bishops and priests made brave and lonely protests but the Church as a whole remained silent throughout the Nazi era. One of the few who spoke out was Cardinal Faulhaber, who met with Hitler on 9 November 1936 and condemned the racial laws and the sterilization programme. Hitler lost his temper and informed Faulhaber that the Church had no business interfering in affairs of state and that he would not tolerate any such attempts. When five months later the Papal encyclical *Mit brennender Sorge* was published and read from the pulpits of churches throughout Germany Hitler exploded. Goebbels orchestrated a smear campaign against the Church in the media and also arrested hundreds of priests and nuns on charges of sexual immorality. They were quickly convicted and sent to concentration camps.

THE CONFESSIONAL CHURCH RESISTS THE NAZIS

Jehovah's Witnesses refused to serve in the armed forces or to co-operate with many other Nazi policies. They were arrested and held in concentration camps where many died. The majority of Protestant churches opposed the attacks on Christianity and often spoke out on specific issues but on the whole their opposition was muted.

An honourable exception was Pastor Martin Niemöller who was so hostile to the 'Aryan Christianity' of Müller's church that he founded a new religious organization, the Confessional Church. Niemöller was a complex and curious character, a former U-boat commander in the First World War and a man who was politically an extreme nationalist and an ardent reactionary. He described the time of the Weimar Republic that preceded Hitler's rise to power as 'years of darkness' and actually joined the Nazi Party in the late 1920s.

Niemöller welcomed Hitler's appointment as Chancellor, declaring that it offered hope to Germany at last and would bring about a 'national revival'. A less likely opponent of Nazism is difficult to imagine and yet it was Niemöller some eighteen months later who broke with the 'German Christians' and set up his own church, declaring it to be the only 'legitimate' Protestant church in Germany.

On 8 November 1934 Niemöller held a rally at Dahlem, a suburb of Berlin. Twenty thousand people attended to hear him and other Confessional Church leaders speak. The authorities had refused permission for the meeting to take place but Niemöller and the crowd defied the ban.

One speaker declared: 'We are fighting against the defamation of Christ and true Christianity. There are false prophets abroad in this land preaching the doctrine of blood and soil and racial mysticism, which we reject.' A manifesto denounced and rejected Müller's 'German Christians' and the meeting ended with a defiant statement by Niemöller. 'For us,' he said, 'it is a question of which master the German Protestants are going to serve. Christ or another.' Everyone present knew that 'another' referred to Hitler.

This was the largest anti-Nazi rally ever held under the Third Reich. Shaken by the open rebellion shown at the meeting the Gestapo began arresting pastors of the church. Niemöller was left alone for the time being but from that moment onwards the regime had him and his followers in their sights. Over the next two years thousands of Confessional Church ministers were arrested and the church had its funds seized and was forbidden to make collections from the congregation. In spite of these difficulties and the open persecution his church faced Niemöller refused to abandon or even tone down his opposition to the Nazi attitudes.

By now Niemöller had moved from a defence of the independence of the churches and opposition to the anti-Christian propaganda of the regime to an outright condemnation of anti-Semitism. This brought more arrests and a counter-statement by Hanns Kerrl, who had replaced the incompetent Müller as head of the 'German Christians'.

Kerrl declared that:

The Party stands on the basis of Positive Christianity, and Positive Christianity is National Socialism. National Socialism is the doing of God's will. God's will reveals itself in German blood.

Responding to the claim that 'Christianity consists in faith in Christ as the Son of God', Kerrl scornfully replied:

> *That makes me laugh. True Christianity is represented by the Party, and the German people are now called by the Party and especially by the Führer to a real Christianity. The Führer is the herald of a new revelation.*

Similar statements were made by the Mayor of Hamburg who declared that 'we can communicate directly to God through Hitler'; by a group of 'German Christians' who stated that 'Hitler's word is God's law'; and by Baldur von Schirach, head of the Hitler Youth, who claimed:

> *the service of Germany appears to us to be genuine and sincere service of God; the banner of the Third Reich appears to us to be His banner; and the Führer of the people is the Saviour whom He sent to rescue us.*

Niemöller would have no truck with such statements which he understandably regarded as blasphemous. In a final show of public defiance on Sunday 27 June 1937 he preached his last sermon. The church was packed to the rafters with worshippers and Niemöller, knowing or at least guessing that this would be his swansong, concluded his sermon with the defiant words:

> *We have no more thoughts of using our own powers to escape the authorities than had the Apostles of God. No more are we ready to keep silent at man's behest when God commands us to speak. For it is, and must remain, the case that we must obey God rather than man.*

Three days later Niemöller was arrested and imprisoned. After eight months of incarceration he was transferred to Sachsenhausen concentration camp where he remained for the next seven years before being liberated by American troops.

Another eight hundred leading ministers and members of the Confessional Church were also arrested and sent to the camps where many of them died. The dangerous resistance to the regime shown by Niemöller and his followers was at an end. Anxious to preserve the remnants of the movement, a leading bishop issued a public statement that 'the National Socialist conception of life is the national and political teaching which determines and characterizes German mankind. As such, it is obligatory upon German Protestants also.' The bishop also ordered his pastors to take a vow of allegiance and obedience to Hitler. By 1938 the Protestant resistance to the Nazis had been utterly crushed.

DIETRICH BONHOEFFER JOINS THE GERMAN RESISTANCE

With the arrest and imprisonment of Niemöller, active defiance by German Protestants to Hitler virtually ceased. A notable exception was Dietrich Bonhoeffer, generally considered one of the outstanding theologians of the twentieth century. Bonhoeffer was in New York as war approached and could easily have remained there for the duration of the conflict. He was urged to do so by many of his friends and colleagues but refused. Instead he reluctantly made the brave decision to return to Germany. He explained to his colleague, the American theologian Reinhold Niebuhr:

Christians in Germany will face the terrible alternative of either willing the defeat of their own nation in order that Christian civilization may survive, or willing the victory of their nation and thereby destroying Christian civilization. I know which of those alternatives I must choose.

Bonhoeffer, along with his brother and brothers-in-law, became active in the German Resistance to Hitler. He managed to survive until 1943 in spite of his increasing involvement in plots against the *Führer*. Possibly his organization had been infiltrated by the SS because he certainly spoke on a visit to Sweden in 1942 about Himmler being in the process of launching a rebellion against Hitler. Whether this was deliberate disinformation by the SS, whether Himmler at that early stage was considering a coup (he certainly did so at a later stage of the war) or whether it was a simple misunderstanding of his intentions, the result was the same. Bonhoeffer was arrested and sent to Buchenwald. In April 1945 he was executed, as were his brother and brothers-in-law. It was a sad end to the life of a brave, brilliant and utterly principled man.

HIMMLER AND NEO-PAGANISM

Himmler was one of the leading supporters of the pagan revival. The worship of Wotan and other Germanic gods was a passion of his and other heathen-minded Germans, both throughout the years before the Nazi Party came to power and once it became the government of the country. Himmler described Christianity as 'the greatest pestilence which could have befallen us in history'. As early as 1934 attempts were made to establish the summer and winter solstices as the principal religious festivals in place of the existing Christian ceremonies. Christmas lights were spoken of as symbolizing the victory of light over the darkness and the process of perpetual renewal in nature through the seasons. Rather than simply lights shining from a tree, the symbol of light burning from large pyres to celebrate the solstice became common. The *Völkischer Beobachter* declared 'holy fires we light to celebrate the turning of the sun, fires that are symbols of the decadent and the bad; fires that are symbols of the new ascent to the light, which means life'. At Ruhlsdorf near Berlin members of the German Labour Front conducted a Yuletide ceremony involving lighting a large pyre while the members lined up before it with blazing torches, an event described by the *Völkischer Beobachter* as 'wonderful knightly scene'.

Wilhelm Kube, Governor of Brandenburg, wrote in *Der Deutsche*:

The Christmas celebration in Germanic lands is not an invention of the Christian church but our forefathers. The day of the winter solstice was holy to our ancestors and the period around the winter solstice was filled with the fairyland magic of the Nordic soul. In this period gifts were exchanged without an indecent hind-thought of getting a reward from heaven in return. The Nordic man did not think of a reward for decent deeds. For us, therefore, even the Christian Christmas remains a festival of Germanic love, Germanic ways and Germanic benevolence.

Children were taught to pray, '*Führer*, my *Führer*, bequeathed to me by the Lord, protect and preserve me as long as I live'. In the Hitler Youth von Schirach was eagerly inculcating pagan principles into the impressionable children under his command; Ley was turning May Day into a ritual for the celebration of the rites of nature; and at Easter 1936 pagan celebrations of *Ostermond* were organized as a deliberate counterweight to the Christian Easter. A large pagan rally was also held at Burg Hunxe in the Rhineland and various pagan bookshops and magazines were flourishing. On the whole these neo-pagan fantasies were generally regarded either as harmless pieces of theatre or as sources of amusement but they were among the aspects of the Nazi regime that aroused the fiercest criticism from the churches.

SAVITRI DEVI AND HINDU INFLUENCES ON NEO-PAGANISM

One of the most interesting Nazi fellow-travellers was Savitri Devi, actually a Greek woman named Maximiani Portas. Devi was a complex character who converted to Hinduism and adopted an extreme and racist form of that religion. At no stage in her life did she ever express any reservations about Nazism and late in her life she became a Holocaust denier. She wrote in her article *National Socialism and Neo-Paganism* about the 'positive Christianity' proposed by Rosenberg, Feder and others before going on to make her own position entirely clear. Devi said:

It is certain that, under all the talk about 'positive Christianity,' there was, from the beginning, in every thoughtful National Socialist, the feeling that Germany in particular and the Aryan world at large need a new religious consciousness, and that the Nazi Movement must sooner or later help it to awake and to express itself.

Bormann, like Rosenberg, did not share the neo-pagan beliefs and attitudes of Himmler and Devi. His principal concern was with the ideological dominance of National Socialism over any competing belief systems or rival power centres. To a considerable extent that was also Hitler's primary purpose in waging his war against the churches, although the *Führer* also had an entirely genuine hatred of Christianity which was largely emotional but partly ideological. As a lapsed Catholic, Hitler hated Protestants more than he hated Catholicism, while with Bormann the reverse was the case. Bormann saw the Pope as a rival claimant for power and allegiance who was an inherent threat to the primacy of the *Führer* whereas to Hitler the Protestant claim for the liberty of the individual conscience represented a greater danger.

For Rosenberg and Himmler, although the perceived threat to the authority of the Nazis was very much a point on which they criticized the churches, their main opposition was rooted in genuine ideological disagreement. Himmler's conscious neo-paganism and the strange inverted sense of ethics he possessed led him to consider Christianity as morally wrong as well as mistaken. Rosenberg, with his vision of the world as inherently evil and a place from which we should all seek to escape, regarded Christianity as a 'world affirming creed'. In his view it prevented the individual from achieving his or her ultimate destiny of surrender and extinction.

Against the fierce integrity of men like Niemöller and Bonhoeffer the Nazis had nothing of comparable weight to offer as a vision. Rosenberg's gloomy view of world renunciation was hardly an inspiring prospect; Himmler's neo-pagan fantasies were not even taken seriously by Hitler. The use of brutal force and even murder did cow Christians in Germany into silence but the fatal flaw that lay at the dark heart of Nazism doomed its attempt to replace a far more

Above all the Nazis were concerned that their symbols of power should be obeyed rather than those of any other organization, and to that end they worked tirelessly on displays of strength.

ancient creed with its own delusions. In a sense the Nazi movement was always dominated by an inner negativity. Nazi ideology was governed by its obsessions with the things it hated far more than the things it professed to admire.

Both National Socialism and Christianity demanded loyalty, faith and adherence to certain ethical principles. The Nazi attempt to supplant Christian belief in the hearts and minds of the German people was conscious, deliberate and aggressive. A questionnaire to the leaders of the *Bund Deutscher Mädel* – the League of German Girls – actually asked if God or Hitler was 'greater, more powerful, and stronger'. In a very real sense the Nazi Party and its institutions were designed to replace the churches as centres of worship. In the place of God stood Hitler; in place of the Devil, the Jews.

As for the ethical side of National Socialism its moral code was little more than an inversion of Christian values. In place of kindness it exalted hardness; in place of a universal sense of humanity it offered a vision of 'Aryans' as the Master Race and Germans as the natural leaders of Aryanism. There was no promise of salvation for all in this barren creed but at best an eternal subservience to Germany as slaves and for the Jews and gypsies physical extermination. That such attitudes could be considered a worthy foundation for any kind of political ideal is astonishing enough; that they could seriously be regarded as religious imperatives defies belief.

The great religions of the world all, in one form or another, offer the prospect of salvation to all true believers regardless of gender, ethnicity or skin colour. Nazism, with its racial exclusiveness and utter fixation upon German dominance, could never be more than a pale shadow of the Christian faith it so resolutely denounced.

What did National Socialism have to offer to non-Germans, still more non-Aryans? A bleak nothingness and the promise of enslavement or extinction. How could such crude notions win genuine allegiance from those not 'fortunate' enough to belong to the privileged group for whom alone salvation was reserved in Nazi eyes?

As Christianity triumphed over the persecution of the Roman emperors who demanded worship as living gods so too it ultimately proved victorious over Hitler's attempt to set himself up in the place of God.

Chapter Four

THE NEW TEUTONIC KNIGHTS

THE ORIGINAL TEUTONIC KNIGHTS flourished during the Middle Ages, leading crusades against the pagan Slavs in Prussia and even as far east as Russia. They saw themselves as warrior missionaries spreading Christianity by fire and sword. The SS as visualized by Himmler was designed as a conscious revival of the earlier order, exemplifying Nazi ideals and helping to disseminate them throughout the world. Himmler genuinely saw the SS as an order of knights motivated by the Nazi 'code of chivalry'.

NAZIS APPROPRIATE THE IMAGE OF THE TEUTONIC KNIGHTS

From the very beginning of the Nazi Party, the power of the symbolic associations of knighthood in general and the Teutonic Knights in particular became a device used by the leadership to attract support. As early as 1920, during the Nazis' first election campaign, a picture of a Teutonic Knight was displayed representing his patriotic desire to protect the eastern regions of Germany from Bolshevist Russia. The knight was represented as being swordless as a symbol of the country's extensive disarmament following its defeat in the First World War. The message of the poster was that although the knight still wished to defend his nation he was no longer able to do so effectively.

Mein Kampf saw the process of mythologizing carried much further. Hitler argued that it was the historic destiny of the German people to expand to the east and the knights, who had conquered Prussia and other parts of Eastern Europe, were held up as images of courage, duty, honour and patriotism.

FOUNDATION OF THE SS

The SS was originally founded as a small unit designed to be Hitler's personal guard. At the time the SA was seen as his main power base within the Party and the SS was regarded as little more than a decorative addition purely for his personal protection. In the beginning it was subject to the authority of the SA and looked upon as very much a junior organization with no real significance.

The appointment of Heinrich Himmler to the position of deputy leader of the SS changed that perception dramatically. Himmler was not a man with a commanding presence and was certainly physically anything but an advert for the supposed Aryan racial ideals of the Party. When he took part in the 1923 Munich Putsch he hardly distinguished himself. He was part of a picket outside the War Ministry whose members were arrested after the police broke it up – with the notable exception of Himmler. Even with a loaded gun he was not considered

Tannhäuser, knight, Minnesänger *and poet of Ancient Germany as depicted in the* Codex Manesse.

important enough to arrest. He caught the train home and brooded over the failure.

As a result of the failed putsch, the SA was banned by the authorities and on his release from prison, Hitler set up the SS to replace it. At the time it was seen as a purely temporary measure but Himmler, who had become secretary to Gregor Strasser, soon changed that. Strasser was a rising man in the Party and widely thought of as a possible alternative leader to Hitler.

The SS had limited duties at that time. As well as being Hitler's bodyguard they also sold advertising for the Party newspaper and gathered information about political opponents. Himmler filed, co-ordinated and analyzed this information to such good effect that he attracted attention at last. In 1925 he was appointed deputy leader of the SS.

HIMMLER TURNS THE SS INTO AN ELITE CORPS

Himmler took his new position very seriously and within a short space of time he had turned his small group into an elite force of men who were smartly turned out, totally disciplined (in stark contrast to the rowdy brawlers of the SA) and completely loyal to the Party and its leader. Hitler's opinion of Himmler's character was no higher than before but he certainly realized that he had underestimated his abilities. The result was permission to expand his SS contingent dramatically and to make him the custodian of the Blood Flag of the Nazi Party. Himmler regarded this as an honour and a sacred trust and by 1929 he had turned his unit, of which he was now the undisputed leader, into the most reliable section of the entire Party mechanism. By 1931 it had become a serious force within the Party. Once Hitler came to power its numbers expanded considerably and in 1934 it was entrusted with the job of purging the unruly SA. From that moment on it became the dominant force in Germany and Himmler the second most powerful man in the country.

To Himmler the SS represented far more than a bodyguard or even an elite fighting force. He saw it as a knightly order devoted to the ideals of Nazism and as much a chivalric order as the ancient medieval knights had been. When Himmler became the leader of the SS, he added an extra layer of mythological and occult fantasies to the existing medieval romantic dreams of German nationalists. He conflated elements of the Knights Templar with the Teutonic Knights as well as adding other aspects derived from various secret societies and magical groups. Himmler saw his new knightly order as the highest expression of Nazi values and his 'new Teutonic Knights' as a modern replacement for the aristocracy that combined the functions of warriors, scholars, educators, priests and rulers. They would be trained in a closed 'order' and work through 'creative action' to dominate and govern the world.

Himmler's obsession with medieval Germany led him to see the SS as an instrument of a revived feudalism with the *Führer* playing the role of king and the members of his dark order as feudal lords, owing allegiance to him but with extensive authority over the rest of the population. The SS was divided into squadrons, each bearing a name with some kind of knightly 'association'.

Himmler's view of the SS as a knightly order was widely shared. The organization was perceived by the majority of Germans as an elite body whose members represented the best of Nazi ideals. During the probationary period before acceptance many candidates were weeded out as unsuitable. Himmler was particularly anxious not to have homosexuals or alcoholics in his ranks, a stark contrast to the far more open membership of the SA. If they completed the training successfully SS applicants swore the *Sippeneid* – the 'kith and kin oath'. The motto of the SS was 'Meine Ehre heisst Treue' – my honour is loyalty. This was also inscribed on the daggers they wore. Rudolf Höss, a leading member of the SS and later commandant of Auschwitz, declared:

We were told all the time we were the elect, we were to be the Führer's and Himmler's special instruments for creating a new Reich. They became our conscience, we lost our personal moral self-determination.

PRINCIPLES AND TRAINING OF THE SS

The principles governing the 'order' were expressly stated to be courage, loyalty, obedience and honour. In the distorted 'idealism' of the Nazi ethos mass murder was seen as a 'sacred duty' and equated with 'self-sacrifice' and 'martyrdom'. Like their medieval precursors the new Teutonic Knights of the SS made war against the Slavs to the east of Germany. The black clothes of the SS aroused more terror than any other Nazi or German uniform, even that of the hated Gestapo. Himmler was proud of the fear the black uniform of his order inspired and worked hard to increase the degree of terrified respect in which it was held.

The SS candidate had to spend a year winning his sports badge before entering the Labour Service and then spending two years in the army. Following an intensive course designed to reinforce his indoctrination and loyalty he would be admitted to full membership. The ceremony of his induction into the SS always took place on 9 November. On that day he went to the *Feldherrnhalle* in Munich and at 10 pm took part in his joining ritual. At this ceremony he swore an oath of perpetual and unconditional loyalty to Hitler. One SS man described the scene:

> Tears came to my eyes when, by the light of the torches, thousands of voices repeated the oath in chorus. It was like a prayer.

THE BLACK HUNDRED

In spite of the relentless conditioning and depersonalization Himmler was always concerned about possible disloyalty. A special inner circle nicknamed the Black Hundred had the task of seeking out any possible doubters or treasonable tendencies within the SS. Robert Ley warned them that:

> He who fails or actually betrays the Party and its *Führer* will not thereby merely be deprived of an office, but he personally, together with his family, his wife, and his children, will be destroyed.

The Leibstandarte Adolf Hitler *at their barracks in Berlin Lichterfelde – this elite SS division was Hitler's personal bodyguard. At the Nuremberg Trials they were found collectively guilty of war crimes committed across Europe.*

When the Australian academic Stephen Roberts questioned some SS members about the Black Hundred he was told that loyalty mattered above all else and that it was necessary for any potential traitors within the organization to be weeded out and dealt with. Even allowing for an understandable reluctance to express doubt to a foreign writer it is almost certain that there were far fewer instances of disloyalty or even disillusionment among the members of the SS than those of any other Nazi organization. Himmler's brainwashing was extremely successful.

THE SS AS AN ARISTOCRACY OF RACE

All roads within the Nazi Party eventually led back to what Hitler once described as the bedrock of his faith, the racial doctrine. Other principles of the Party might be jettisoned altogether or suspended periodically before returning but the overriding primacy of anti-Semitism and the exaltation of Aryanism was one 'principle' that Hitler never abandoned or modified. The demonization of Jews reached such levels of absurdity that it is incredible that they were ever believed and yet the notion of them as subhuman cartoon-like villains devoid of all redeeming features was relentlessly drummed into the heads of the German people.

Against these mythical demons stood the noble Aryan. In the same way that the original Teutonic Knights required candidates seeking admission to their order to provide proof of pure aristocratic blood for eight generations on both sides of their family so within the ranks of the SS it was necessary for members to provide proof of 'pure Aryan blood' going back three generations. The SS may have substituted an aristocracy of race for a literal nobility of blood but in essence the principle remained the same, an elite governing the majority of the population. Himmler knew exactly what he expected of his black-coated knights.

The fact that the aristocratic principle within the SS rested upon race rather than class offered new opportunities for social mobility. Lower middle-class and working-class people began to join the SS partly as a means of advancing their status and careers. Candidates wishing to join the SS had to undergo a rigorous, brutal training programme of two years before they were admitted to the 'knightly order' and upon joining they had to swear a solemn oath of loyalty, unquestioning obedience and fidelity. As a result of the two-year probationary period before they were accepted into the order they had already become deeply imbued with its ideology and its values and had developed the type of character and adopted the style of behaviour expected of them as members by the time they finally joined.

THE DESTRUCTION OF INDIVIDUALITY

The SS offered its recruits a vision of a golden future with the racial aristocrats ruling the world. To become part of this utopia it was necessary to abandon independence of thought and action or even all individuality. This sacrifice of the self was justified on the grounds that it led to the development of the 'new man'.

Other aspects of the SS mentality were an idealized concept of nature and contempt for rationality. The SS man was expected to 'think with his blood' rather than using his brain and the existing moral compass was turned on its head. Nietzsche spoke in an entirely different context and with a meaning far removed from the sense in which the Nazis misappropriated his phrase, 'the transvaluation of all values'. In the ethical universe inhabited by the SS such a 'transvaluation' really did take place. Compassion was despised as weakness; cruelty was glossed over as 'hardness'; the notion of human dignity was replaced with total contempt for 'inferiors'; and 'comradeship' was valued above love or family ties.

These men were brought to this state of mind through a relentless and brutal training programme. Their own psychological and physical bullying at the hands of their instructors destroyed their personality and turned them into desensitized robots, incapable of a single spontaneous human emotion. There was even a term coined for the mental state of the SS man: *Kadavergehorsam* – 'corpse obedience'. Men were drilled for hours on end, compelled to crawl through pipes and narrow spaces, made to navigate obstacle courses and forced to march for long distances without food or water. They were taught to be silent, to fight off dogs without any weapons and to balance on their helmets a grenade from which the pin had been removed until it exploded.

There was also the psychological conditioning, a relentless mixture of racial mythology, meditations on the 'race soul', the study of genealogy, of German history and various forms of visualization that were adapted from Loyola's *Spiritual Exercises*. Under the triple pressures of psychological brainwashing, physical abuse and a desperate desire to become part of a knightly order creating a racial utopia, the character of the SS man was formed. He committed himself unconditionally to the service of the order for the rest of his life. An SS man abandoned any sense of selfhood to become part of the wider 'knightly' community of the organization. The Nazi leader Robert Ley when addressing some SS recruits commented 'externally you already look alike and in a short time you will be alike inside as well'.

PHYSICAL REQUIREMENTS OF SS MEN

The physical similarities of the men were not accidental. Himmler laid down extremely strict criteria for admission to the order requiring that candidates must be at least 1.7 metres tall (5 feet 7 inches) although if they were over 1.8 metres (5 feet 11 inches) their height had to be proportionate to their body mass. The size of hands and thighs, the way they walked, the degree of body hair, even the extent to which they sweated, were all assessed for the individual's suitability for admission to the order. Before they even reached this stage of evaluation Himmler personally studied the photographs of the candidates.

If they passed this initial screening they were tested physically, psychologically and in terms of their political soundness. They had to show proof that there were no genetic defects in their family tree and to submit to an examination for 'racial purity' by a panel of 'race experts', doctors and SS officers.

ENGAGEMENT AND MARRIAGE DECREE

The racial requirements demanded of SS men did not end even when they were approved as members of the organization. Himmler's vision of them as an aristocracy of race led him to control every aspect of their lives. The notorious 'Engagement and Marriage Decree' of 31 December 1931 required every member who wished to marry to obtain consent from the Race Office of the SS. Article 4 of this decree stated expressly that 'marriage consent will be granted and denied solely and exclusively on the criteria of race and hereditary health'. The requirements for the approval of the proposed marriage meant that not only the men had to be 'racially healthy'. Prospective brides had to demonstrate their own physical and mental health, give their family's medical history and submit to a medical examination, assessment and measurements in order to establish their conformity to the Aryan ideal of womanhood.

In addition to these requirements would-be brides had to provide a family tree showing no Jewish, Slavonic, black or Asiatic ancestors, if possible as far back as five generations. All of these names as well as those of the bride and groom were then entered into the 'Table of Ancestors' which was then placed in the record of the Race Office.

In spite of the overwhelmingly male and militaristic ethos of his order Himmler was deeply troubled by the excessively masculine nature of German society in general and the SS in particular. 'We militarize impossible things,' he said in an address to his *Gruppenführers* on 18 February 1937. This extraordinary tirade denounced homosexuality; logical thinking – especially with regard to women; the oppression and undervaluation of women; Christianity, which he equated with homosexuality; the witch craze; and 'female tyranny', which he believed existed throughout the United States.

EGALITARIANISM OF THE SS

In spite of the openly feudal nature of the SS there was paradoxically a fierce egalitarianism within its ranks. Officers enjoyed absolute and unquestionable authority over, and obedience from, the men under their command but they were strictly forbidden to abuse their power or derive personal gain from their position. Naturally some SS men *did* break these rules but if their transgressions came to Himmler's attention the guilty individual was demoted, expelled or even sent to a concentration camp. The strange scale of values within the organization was clearly exemplified by Himmler's indifference to the suffering of others and yet his indignation at financial corruption. In his distorted scheme of things, the SS 'knights' had a sacred trust to 'purify' the world through, among other things, the murder of 'inferior races' but they also had to display a total resistance to the ordinary temptations of their position such as financial gain.

The Nazi policy of *Schein* – appearance – meant that ideals, ceremonies, traditions and training were employed extensively to command absolute, unquestioning and instinctive allegiance to the doctrines and instructions of the Nazi regime and its ideology. In no area of German life was this process more fully realized than among the ranks of the SS. Himmler taught them that they were a knightly order charged with a sacred mission and that only by following their 'quest' to the bitter end could they achieve the bizarre 'redemption' that Nazi values afforded to someone who 'did their job well'.

What the Nazis in general and the SS in particular sought to achieve was the utter destruction of individuality and an entirely collective sense of consciousness. The nation and the race were of primary importance and the individual's duty was to be an unquestioning cog within a vast machine, playing his or her allotted part within the wider whole. The concept of an 'organic' society was put forward as a superior model to the 'fragmented' and 'atomized' model that the Nazis claimed was the result of liberalism. They focused their attention upon developing a type of member who was essentially an efficient but wholly depersonalized unit within a team, utterly incapable of independent thought or action.

THE SS INNER CIRCLE

The inner circle of leadership within the SS was made up of twelve individuals. They were Karl Wolff, *Persönlicher Stab Reichsführer* SS; Gottlob Berger, SS *Hauptamt*; Hans Jüttner, SS *Führungshauptamt*; Richard Walther Darré, *Rasse-und Siedlungshauptamt*; Paul Scharfe, *Hauptamt* SS-*Gericht*; Walter Schmitt, SS-*Personalhauptamt*; Reinhard Heydrich, *Reichssicherheitshauptamt*; Kurt Daluege, *Hauptamt Ordnungspolizei*; Oswald Pohl, SS-*Wirtschafts-und Verwaltungshauptamt*; August Heissmeyer, *Dienststelle SS-Obergruppenführer*; Werner Lorenz, *Hauptamt Volksdeutsche Mittelstelle*; and Ulrich Greifelt, *Hauptamt Reichskommissar für die Festigung deutschen Volkstums*. These men, together with Himmler himself, made up the inner sanctum of thirteen, a figure that many speculate was not chosen arbitrarily but precisely because of its anti-Christian associations. Certainly Himmler regarded witches as German heroines who had been martyred by the Catholic Church and who deserved to be honoured rather than condemned. He may well have consciously determined on the traditional number for a witches' coven when establishing his own inner circle of initiates.

The Nazi emphasis on tradition, public festivals and a communal approach to life was particularly pronounced within the SS. In addition to Teutonic and Norse myths the Arthurian legends and particularly the story of the Holy Grail profoundly influenced Himmler to the point of obsession. They played a key role in drawing up the rituals for the SS and the insignia they wore and Himmler's pursuit of holy relics became a mania. He attempted to design the headquarters of his order in direct imitation of the Round Table and as a conscious homage to the Arthurian legends.

THE SS AND PUBLIC FESTIVALS

Deliberate attempts were made to mythologize as many areas of German life as possible and to associate them in every conceivable way with the Nazi Party. From 1924 onwards there was an annual celebration of the failed Munich Putsch in 1923 during which the 'Blood Flag' was presented for an almost religious veneration.

In 1925 Himmler commissioned a replica of the Spear of Destiny which he insisted on keeping by his bedside as he slept. It was later transferred to Wewelsburg Castle.

Key dates in the year were focused on celebrating specifically 'Nordic' or Nazi events or symbols. The Nazi 'year' began on 30 January when Hitler was appointed Chancellor and made an announcement of 'what I [Hitler] took over and what I have done with the power entrusted to me'. The day concluded with the induction of eighteen-year-old Hitler Youth members into full membership of the Party. On 24 February the 'annunciation' – a word with deliberately religious overtones – of the twenty-five point programme of the Nazi Party was commemorated. Then on 18 March there was a memorial ceremony

Jesus on the Cross and the Spear of Destiny: Himmler was obsessed with the story of the Holy Grail and the pursuit of holy relics became a mania for him.

for those who had died during the First World War, including a performance of the second movement of Beethoven's Third Symphony. On 20 April Hitler's birthday was celebrated and the day closed with an army parade through the Brandenburg Gate. This was followed by 1 May, Workers' Day, when the Party emphasized its 'oneness' with the working classes, Hitler's welfare state policies and the socialist aspects of National Socialism. The summer solstice festival was an important date in the SS calendar and on the neo-pagan wing of the Nazis but it attracted much less public interest.

The September celebration was different and was perhaps the most popular of all the Nazi festivals. It was the week-long Party Rally at Nuremberg that took place during the first week of September. Around half a million people attended the rally on average and in 1938 almost a million were present. Hans Frank wrote:

> *In that week-long hymn of jubilation, colours, lights, music and festivities nobody thought 'ideologically', 'programmatically' or 'objectively-politically'.*

The end of September saw the Harvest Festival where 50,000 agricultural workers and farmers marched to the Bückerberg and placed a giant wheat sheaf in the shape of a crown.

Then between 8–9 November the failed Munich Putsch of 1923 was commemorated, an event as solemn as the September rally was joyful. All these events were turned into public festivities with overtly religious overtones.

The solstice ceremonies were celebrations particularly close to Himmler's heart. Through his influence they became an integral part of the SS year. The summer festival included prizes for the winners of the SS sporting contest, girls dancing and games for both boys and girls. At the winter solstice the emphasis was on the past and upon honouring ancestors. Himmler stated that 'a *Volk* that honours its ancestors will always have children; only those *Völker* who know no ancestors are childless'.

BAPTISMS AND WEDDINGS

Among the SS itself baptisms and weddings were carried out following the ceremonies laid down by Himmler. His 'new Teutonic Knights' were indoctrinated with Nazi 'values' at every possible opportunity and through every stage of their life.

Race and sex were frequently blended together in Himmler's obsessional fantasies about 'selective breeding'. His pursuit of the

Nuremberg rallies took place in the first week of September – each one was stage-managed to top previous events: in 1933, there was a giant eagle and Hitler on the rostrum.

chimaera of the Master Race led him to make a huge number of speeches on the subject. One of the more bizarre examples is his address on 8 November 1936 to senior SS leaders. In this extraordinary speech he remarked that a man might feel obligated towards a girl he had been seeing for a few months but simple affection was not enough to make her a suitable partner. Himmler declared that she might have a brother or uncle who suffered from mental illness. He added:

> *The SS man may never act without decency, on the contrary we must say openly, 'I am sorry, I cannot marry you, because there have been many major diseases in your family.'*

Himmler went on to assert that because of 'the false and stupid views of three centuries', the marriage permission was necessary.

Newly married couples were each given a silver beaker. At the birth ceremonies that took the place of baptisms within the SS and with which Himmler ultimately intended to replace all christenings the child received a silver tankard and a *Lebensband* – the 'life band' – which was a large ribbon of blue silk that was wrapped around him or her at the ceremony. His or her name was then entered into the birth book and the Family Book of the SS. The mother then received a silver spoon. Finally the birth ring was produced, ceremonial words were spoken in an act of blessing the ring and the child was named. The parents and sponsors – Himmler's version of godparents – were instructed to raise the child with a 'true, brave, German heart according to the will of God'.

THE LEBENSBORN

Himmler's most ambitious attempt to bring together his views on sex and race was the *Lebensborn* (fountain of life) project. This was instituted in December 1935 and initially placed under the Race Office of the SS. It was an organization that originally set out to care for unmarried mothers with 'pure blood' who had been made pregnant by SS men or police officers. The intention was to allow them to give birth in private and then either to place the children with an SS family wishing to adopt or put pressure on the father to marry the girl.

The first *Lebensborn* home opened in 1936 at Steinhöring near Munich. It was soon serving other clients besides its intended original base. Before long aristocratic women went to the home surreptitiously to give birth to unwanted children that were then adopted. SS men also began to use it as a place to conduct affairs with suitably Aryan females and even wives of SS officers began to use it as a maternity home.

Both fathers and mothers were subjected to rigorous investigation by the Race Office and only allowed to enter the *Lebensborn* programme if they fulfilled its strict racial criteria. Himmler became involved in every detail of the organization of the *Lebensborn*. He placed runic symbols on its stationery, concerned himself with the decoration of the homes and

A Lebensborn baptism with three SS men and a photo of Hitler above a table bedecked with a swastika: the Lebensborn breeding programme took Nazi ideology to its (il)logical conclusion with unhappiness guaranteed for all parties.

the diet of the girls – he was particularly keen that the day should begin with porridge – as well as the duration of their confinement. In 1938 he removed the *Lebensborn* from the control of the Race Office and took it under his direct supervision.

Himmler believed that procreation could no longer be thought of as a matter of private choice but was instead an activity that needed to be directed and regulated by the state. Pregnancies outside marriage were positively encouraged both as a way of boosting the birth rate and as a means of providing more male children to become future soldiers. In line with this philosophy the *Lebensborn* organization looked after unmarried mothers and fostered out illegitimate children. Himmler believed this would radically drive up the birth rate and to some extent it did. SS officers were compelled to join the *Lebensborn* organization and support it financially through deductions from their pay.

Himmler encouraged his SS disciples to participate in the programme, declared that it was their duty as 'valuable and racially pure men' to act as 'conception assistants' and thus become 'the basis for a new advance of the Germanic race'. Adding new layers of bizarre occult fantasy, he announced that babies who were conceived in an 'Aryan cemetery' would be filled with the ancestral spirits of 'the dead heroes who lay therein' and actually published lists of suitable cemeteries in *Das Schwarze Korps*, the SS magazine.

Girls were positively encouraged to join the *Lebensborn* programme, both through exhortation and benefits. They were given financial inducements of 1,000 *Reichsmarks* to become mothers and were also exempted from Labour Service duty. The slogan 'present the *Führer* with a child' was constantly presented to German women as an honourable ideal and a practical way of demonstrating their patriotism and loyalty. Members of the *Bund Deutscher Mädel* (League of German Girls) were particularly exhorted to join the programme.

After the conquest of Poland the *Lebensborn* project was expanded by kidnapping children of racially suitable Poles. Once the invasion of the USSR began the same process took place with Soviet children.

In these activities the SS was deeply involved and just as it had turned the original conception of the *Lebensborn* organization from maternity homes for unmarried mothers into a stud farm so too it became involved in kidnapping and murder to perpetuate Himmler's racial mythology.

HIMMLER'S ATTITUDE TO RELIGION

It is ironic that the first question asked of an SS candidate was whether or not he believed in God. If he was unwise enough to give a negative answer his application to join the order was refused immediately. As Himmler told a group of farmers in November 1935:

> be assured one cannot be incorporated between ancestors and children in an – according to human ideas – eternal past and the – for human calculation so long as this star Earth exists – eternal future of our people if one does not believe in deepest humility in a Godly ruler and a God-given order for man.

Himmler tapped into and diverted the religious impulses of these overwhelmingly young and idealistic people. He made them believe they were a knightly order leading the front line of the crusade for the salvation of Germany. They had a profound sense of purpose, duty and belonging which deserved a worthier cause. The SS men gladly sacrificed the burdens of freedom and individuality for the false gods of nation, race and Nazi ideology. To a greater degree than any other part of the Third Reich's machinery of state the SS were incapable of independent thought or action. They had been so thoroughly dehumanized, brainwashed and indoctrinated that they had completely lost any kind of capacity to question, still less to dispute, the things they were taught and those that they were eventually commanded to do. Their inner core of steely determination made it impossible for them to feel any sense of horror or shame at the atrocities so many of them committed. As a typical SS man answered on being questioned by the Allies, 'I have no opinion; I obey.'

One of the questions in the SS 'catechism' was the following:

Q: Why do you obey?
A: From inner conviction, from belief in Germany, in the Führer, *in the Movement and in the SS, and from loyalty.*

With such a mindset, where rigidity, dogmatism and tunnel vision were enshrined to a degree that made the severest military discipline appear almost liberal, it is no accident that Himmler's 'new Teutonic Knights' became, like their medieval precursors, apostles who spread their beliefs through murder and destruction. Himmler's dark neo-pagan visions and occult fantasies led to the mental, emotional and spiritual corruption of an entire generation.

Chapter Five

THE NAZI GRAIL CASTLE

MANY MYTHS HAVE GROWN up around Wewelsburg Castle and its associations with Himmler. Some are easily disproved, others implausible but in spite of the most rigorous sceptical investigation a small but undeniable kernel of truth remains. The gap between Himmler's conception of the castle and its role, as opposed to the reality of what he could and could not do in his fortress, was undoubtedly a topic that vexed him. In a very real sense the creation of Wewelsburg represented the fulfilment of his dreams – one might as well say fantasies – to the same extent that the castle of Neuschwanstein symbolized the romantic vision of the mad King Ludwig of Bavaria. Neuschwanstein survived its founder and continues to be a tourist attraction; Wewelsburg did not and it was many years before Himmler's once proud fortress was restored and opened to the public.

EARLY HISTORY OF WEWELSBURG CASTLE

Wewelsburg Castle lies in the hills of the North Rhine-Westphalia province of Germany near the town of Paderborn, with the nearest large city being Hanover. A castle has stood on the site since the time of Charlemagne but the present structure was built in the early seventeenth century for the bishops of Paderborn, who had owned it since 1301.

The earliest castle on the site was used by Charlemagne and the Holy Roman Emperors who succeeded him as a defensive fortification against the Hungarians. At this time the castle was known as Wifilisburg but by the late tenth century it had fallen into disuse as the Hungarians no longer posed a threat. In 1123 Earl Friedrich von Arnsberg built a new castle on the site but because he was unpopular with his tenant farmers it was destroyed by them on his death in 1124. In 1301 Graf von Waldeck sold the land to the Prince Bishop of Paderborn and at that time there were two fortified buildings on the site, the Bürensche and the Waldecksche-haus. In the early seventeenth century the bishops of Paderborn combined the two fortresses into a single triangular castle. During the Thirty Years War Swedish troops destroyed it and it was not until 1654 that the programme of rebuilding began. This time new features were added with the three towers of the castle being crowned with domes in the baroque architectural style that was fashionable at the time.

The site also had a dark side with a room formerly used by the Inquisition still surviving in the basement. Thousands of witches were held in the castle and tortured and executed. Two trials of witches are known to have taken place there in 1631 but because a confession was said to remove the need for court proceedings most of the condemned witches never received a trial at all. Even after the persecution of witches finally ended the castle continued to house a prison and it was not until 1802 that the prison cells fell into disuse.

In 1802 the castle passed into the hands of the King of Prussia. He neglected it and in January 1815 the North Tower was struck by

Wewelsburg in 1938, four years after restoration work began: the interior was inscribed throughout with runes and Germanic symbols at the behest of Himmler.

lightning and virtually destroyed. Only the outer walls survived the fire. In 1924 it passed into the hands of the district of Büren who turned it into a cultural centre and local museum. The new building included a restaurant and a youth hostel. The North Tower continued to need repair work and during the winter of 1932–3 it was necessary to support it with guy wires. A society for the preservation of the castle took charge of its upkeep but with growing economic difficulties they were less and less able to carry out the degree of renovation that was necessary.

WEWELSBURG AS THE HEADQUARTERS OF HIMMLER'S KNIGHTLY ORDER

From the moment he became leader of the SS, Himmler's conception of the organization was as far more than a bodyguard or even an elite police force. 'Never forget,' he said, 'we are a knightly order.' His fascination with German history, the Arthurian legends and the medieval notions of chivalry was most clearly expressed in the 'Grail Castle' that became the headquarters for the elite of the new 'knightly order'.

Himmler had dreamed of creating such a centre for some years before the appointment of Hitler as Chancellor in 1933 made it possible for his vision to be turned into reality. From that moment, using his new authority as Germany's police chief, he travelled across the country in search of the ideal location for his 'Grail Castle'.

HIMMLER'S 'RASPUTIN', KARL MARIA WILIGUT

In 1933 the castle was drawn to Himmler's attention and he immediately became intrigued by it. It was on 3 November 1933 that Himmler paid his first visit to Wewelsburg Castle. He was accompanied by Karl Maria Wiligut who for six years became one of the *Reichsführer*'s most influential gurus. Wiligut drew Himmler's attention to a nineteenth century poem, *Am Birkenbaum* by Ferdinand Freilingrath. The poet described a battle between invaders from the east and the Germans, who successfully defended their homeland against the enemy. Wiligut suggested that the setting for the battle was in the region of Wewelsburg, an idea that attracted Himmler greatly.

Wiligut had been introduced to Himmler earlier that year and he took the SS leader to the castle, which was now deteriorating after years of neglect. He pointed out a number of reasons why he felt it would be the ideal location for the headquarters of Himmler's order. In the first place, as the former seat of the bishops of Paderborn it had mystical associations with Germany's Christian heritage. Secondly, the bishops had been active and enthusiastic persecutors of witches during the seventeenth century and were responsible for the deaths of 100,000 accused women in their area alone. Many of them had been executed within the castle itself.

THE EXTERNSTEINE

Nearby stood the Externsteine, a natural rock formation that had been a place of worship from as long ago as the time of the Stone Age. Most importantly of all it stood in the region of the Teutoburg Forest, site of the great battle in which the German tribes under their leader

Hermann had defeated the Roman legions sent to conquer them and had slain their commander.

The Externsteine has been described as Germany's equivalent of Ayers Rock. It is actually a rock formation that consists of a series of pillars that protrude out of the surrounding forest. There are five pillars in all with the tallest being 37.5 metres (123 feet) high and they form a natural wall several hundred metres long.

Stone tools have been discovered on the site dating back to at least 10,000BC. It has long been regarded as an important religious centre although there is no actual proof of any kind of pagan activity before the early Christian era. The heathen Saxons certainly did conduct some kind of rituals at the scene and after he conquered them in AD772 Charlemagne forcibly converted them to Christianity. He cut down the Irminsul, a large tree that was a centre of worship for the pagans and whose precise location remains unknown. The most probable site for it is Obermarsberg, formerly known as Eresburg. This is a hill to the south of the Externsteine and tradition asserts that a church dedicated to St Peter was built where the Irminsul had previously stood.

The Externsteine, five large sandstone pillars that, some claim, were once the site of pagan rituals, were labelled as a 'sacred grove' by the Nazis.

From 1920 onwards Wilhelm Teudt began researching German culture in Detmold. He came to the conclusion that the Irminsul was situated close by the Externsteine. Teudt joined the Nazis in 1933 and urged that the Externsteine be turned into a sacred grove to commemorate the Teutonic ancestors of the German nation. Himmler was impressed by Teudt's ideas and founded an Externsteine Foundation in the same year. The *Ahnenerbe* soon devoted considerable time and effort to researching the rocks.

The Externsteine also contains a number of Christian carvings, most notably the Descent from the Cross. This shows Jesus at the Cross together with the Virgin Mary, Joseph of Arimathea and Nicodemus. God, the sun and the moon are all pictured above Jesus while below the Cross a bent tree was said by the pagans to symbolize the Irminsul. On Hitler's birthday and at the summer and winter solstices the Hitler Youth gathered at the Externsteine to sing pagan chants.

On the left-hand side of the Church of St Peter is a stone near the confessional. It is labelled Irminsul and was 'discovered' on the site in 1938. There is no doubt that this cannot be the original Irminsul as it is made out of stone while the sacred object cut down by Charlemagne was a tree. It is however claimed that in a small chapel underneath the altar the original Irminsul once stood. What is virtually certain is that the 1938 'discovery' was a fraud perpetuated on behalf of the *Ahnenerbe* to reinforce the site's pagan associations. Wiligut is considered the most likely author of this particular deception.

As well as its religious significance for both Christians and pagans there is also clear evidence that part of the Externsteine's function was as an astronomical calendar. The rocks contain a twenty-inch window which at the time of the summer solstice aligns with the sun at the moment of sunrise.

As well as the Externsteine itself, the surrounding Teutoburg Forest was also of considerable interest to Himmler and his *Ahnenerbe*. It is a range of low, densely wooded mountains in the North Rhine-Westphalia region of Germany. In AD9 it was the scene of a bloody battle between the German chief Hermann (called Arminius by the Romans) and the Roman legions. The Germans won the battle and during the Napoleonic Wars the victory became a sign of German resistance to foreign invasion and a symbol of national identity. A statue known as the Hermannsdenkmal (Hermann Monument) was erected to commemorate Hermann's triumph. In 1875 Kaiser Wilhelm I dedicated the monument to the nation and added a statue of himself to the north of the forest, at a place known as Porta Westfalica. It was situated on the Wittekindsberg, a hill in the Wiehen Hills mountain range, to commemorate Wilhelm's status as the first ruler of a unified Germany.

The combination of historical, legendary and mystical associations captivated Himmler and when Wiligut also suggested that the castle must have been the site of the battle mentioned in Freilingrath's poem he was convinced.

HIMMLER TAKES OVER WEWELSBURG

The castle was immediately taken over by the SS on a hundred year lease at a nominal rent of one mark a year. Himmler immediately instituted a programme of extensive rebuilding and renovation. He laid the foundation stone of Wewelsburg himself. As work began the castle slowly evolved and became both a reconstructed medieval fortress and a place of spiritual communion. Wewelsburg included a chapel, a private meditation cloister and a library of over twelve thousand books. Himmler also planned a vast triptych painting to demonstrate his ideas on the role of the order.

His instructions to the painter intended to carry out this commission asked him to depict:

a)   The attack of an SS troop in war, in which I envisage the
     representation of a dead or mortally wounded SS man, who
     is married, to show that from death itself and despite it
     new life springs.

A mass celebration of all things Germanic in 1925 near the monument to Hermann, who defeated the Romans in the battle of the Teutoburg Forest near Wewelsburg.

b)   A field in a new land being ploughed by a defence-corps farmer, an SS man.

c)   The newly founded village with the families and numerous children.

Every room within Wewelsburg was furnished in a completely individual style with not a single piece of furniture, ornament or decorative feature being uniform. Frischauer describes how:

Not even a single desk was duplicated. Only leading craftsmen of every branch had been employed to produce fine tapestries, solid oak furniture, wrought-iron door handles, candlesticks. Priceless carpets were acquired, curtains of heavy brocade flanked the high windows. Doors were carved and embellished with precious metals and stones. Built in the old Germanic style on a triangular foundation the burg's towers rose high over the surrounding forest.

HIMMLER AND GERMAN HEROES

Himmler laid down that each room should be named after and associated with Germanic heroes of the past and in some way reflect their lives and achievements. There were rooms dedicated to Charlemagne, Heinrich the Fowler, Otto the Great, Henry the Lion, Philip of Swabia, Frederick Barbarossa, Frederick of Hohenstaufen, Conrad IV and other famous German rulers. The Barbarossa room was reserved for Hitler and the Heinrich the Fowler chamber for Himmler. In the Heinrich the Fowler room Himmler kept the replica of the Spear of Destiny lying on a faded cushion of red velvet and enclosed within a case of antique leather. Himmler frequently held 'conversations' with what he believed to be the spirit of Heinrich the Fowler and declared that he received 'advice' from the man he believed to be his own ancestor. He was fond of saying 'in this case King Heinrich would have acted as follows'.

Himmler remained obsessed with Heinrich the Fowler throughout his period in power. In 1936 he celebrated the thousandth anniversary of the king's death with a festival of remembrance in Quedlinburg, which was a town founded by Heinrich that nestled in the Harz Mountains. The following year Himmler disinterred the king's bones and reburied them in the crypt of Quedlinburg Cathedral. In 1938 he founded the King Heinrich Memorial Foundation for the purpose of reviving 'the spirit and deeds of the king in our time'. On 2 July each year Himmler held a midnight ritual in the crypt to commemorate the birth of the king. Himmler felt a particular identification with this monarch as he had checked the progress of Slav invaders and made Germany strong enough for his son Otto to become Holy Roman Emperor. Like his hero, Himmler consciously saw himself as resisting the 'Asiatic hordes' and as the leader of a 'Crusade for German expansion in the East'.

Himmler seemed to see himself as the reincarnation of Heinrich the Fowler, seen here with the banner of Archangel Michael, founding Europe's first castle, Albrechtsburg.

No expense was spared in the work of reconstructing and renovating Wewelsburg. The rooms contained jewels, suits of armour, shields, swords and even clothes that had been associated in some way with each of the figures to whom they were dedicated. The walls were decorated with rich tapestries and hung with paintings. Himmler also told the architects that he wanted a Gobelin tapestry 'with the figure of a fully developed virginal girl, a future mother' and on the facing wall to be carved in stone 'the figure of a mother with a half-grown lad who is becoming a man'.

INITIAL PLANS FOR WEWELSBURG

Himmler's initial plan was to turn Wewelsburg into a 'Reich school for SS leaders', where officers would receive advanced ideological training. The courses that were originally designed to be taught at the castle were archaeology, prehistory and mythology. All these subjects were given a heavily German orientation. Under the influence of Wiligut, Himmler's vision for Wewelsburg changed and he came to look upon it as the centre of his 'knightly order' and the spiritual focus for all Aryans. In his mind it was a site that would become as sacred as Rome, Glastonbury or Jerusalem.

In Wewelsburg Castle senior SS officers came together to discuss and share their dark ideals. Sometimes a new candidate would be initiated in what was nicknamed 'the ceremony of the stifling air', from the charged psychological atmosphere in which it took place. The dining room at Wewelsburg measured 30.5 by 44 metres (100 by 145 feet) and around the oak 'round table' the SS officers sat on high-backed chairs covered in pigskin with each officer's name engraved on a silver plate that hung from the back of the chair.

When they stayed at Wewelsburg, the SS officers were deliberately given a different room each time in order to enable them to become familiar with the atmosphere of the castle as a whole, the individual history of the historical figures to whom each room was dedicated and the part that the Spear of Destiny had played in the life of each man.

Unemployed German workers began excavating the moat of the castle but before long they were replaced by concentration camp labourers. A total of 3,900 of them worked on the project, 1,285 of them dying during its construction. Originally they were professional criminals who had been set to work but with the outbreak of war gypsies were sent to labour on the project. Following the start of hostilities against the Soviet Union, Russian prisoners of war were also forced to work on the building of Wewelsburg. They were treated with appalling cruelty because of their supposed racial inferiority and most died after only a few months of their forced labour. Their bodies were burned in the camp crematorium and their ashes scattered and used as fertilizer for the camp garden. Himmler took no account of the human cost of building his grand design; all that mattered to him was the realization of his 'vision'.

The architect in charge of renovating Wewelsburg made the main focus of his design the North Tower. He laid out the ground floor in the form of an isosceles triangle, resulting in the Wewelsburg area being shaped like a spear. Himmler of course slept in his room at the castle with a replica of the Spear of Destiny at his bedside. Further evidence of the mystical function of the castle is demonstrated by the fact that even the architects working on the project described it as 'the centre of the world'.

It also stood on a nexus of ley lines, which was another occult preoccupation of Himmler and the 'Occult Bureau' that he ran. In the crypt of Wewelsburg, under a series of arches, stood a black marble altar with the letters SS engraved upon it in silver. There Himmler and his disciples gathered to carry out a number of occult ceremonies. They meditated on honour, the power of race and the imminent arrival of the 'New Man'.

In the crypt was set a circular vault with twelve seats, one for each of the twelve SS initiates who came here. There was a table which was consciously intended as an analogy with the Round Table and in its centre was a flame. The ceiling of the crypt displayed a swastika design set inside a sun wheel; the emblem has been often referred to as a 'black sun'. There was a golden disc in the centre of it but that was removed when Himmler ordered Wewelsburg to be demolished at the end of the war. The SS *Totenkopfring* (Death's Head ring) was designed by Wiligut who advised Himmler extensively on the 'correct' rituals and practices to be carried out at the castle. When an SS officer died, his *Totenkopfring* was taken to Wewelsburg and buried within the castle.

Himmler and his acolytes carried ceremonial daggers, wore silver signet rings and dressed in black uniforms. 'Experts' from the *Ahnenerbe* drew up coats of arms for Himmler and the SS leaders even though hardly any of them had the slightest drop of aristocratic blood flowing through their veins. The castle was the place where Himmler liked to go to escape from the administration of the Gestapo, the police, the SS and the concentration camps. In his inner sanctum of Wewelsburg he could concentrate fully on the 'spiritual' side of his 'mission', surrounded by like-minded initiates of his dark order.

THE DEVELOPMENT OF HIMMLER'S IDEOLOGY AT WEWELSBURG

An entire 'philosophy' was evolved by Himmler during his visits to Wewelsburg. Not only did his racial mythology harden into stone but his inner convictions about secret 'energies' that lay within the earth, which if mastered could lead to the domination of the world, also grew more and more pronounced. He and his inner circle at the castle spent hours pursuing 'magical' methods of controlling people and events.

As well as Himmler himself, one of the principal figures in the Nazi era of Wewelsburg was Manfred von Knobelsdorff, captain of the castle. He was a friend of Wiligut's and he not only repeatedly carried out various rituals designed to invoke the spirit of the Irminsul but also more normal ceremonies such as a baptism attended by Heydrich.

Just as the SS was seen as an order of chivalry so Wewelsburg was looked on as the centre of the rituals, ceremonies and theology of the order. The castle was deliberately laid out like a temple and the crypt became the 'holy of holies' where only the most privileged SS leaders were allowed to visit. In time it would also be designed to hold their ashes and coats of arms. The centre of the crypt was intended to hold an 'eternal flame' in their memory, though the pressures of war meant that this particular part of the project was never completed.

Wewelsburg rapidly became nicknamed 'Black Camelot' by other Nazi Party members. It was never entirely completed largely because of the war but by 1939 it had become the venue for many of the more secretive rituals and bizarre ceremonies of Himmler and the SS.

PUBLIC CEREMONIES IN THE CASTLE

A number of public ceremonies took place in the castle including SS weddings, baptisms of children born in the *Lebensborn* breeding programme and the winter solstice festival with which Himmler wanted to replace Christmas, as well as the midsummer solstice celebration that he wished to be the main event of the annual calendar. The mystical rites and doctrines that he tried to inculcate into the SS were more than mere empty phrases or gestures. Participating in them made those who took part feel even more privileged and part of a mystical fraternity with special duties and responsibilities. They induced a state bordering upon mystical rapture in the devotees who participated, the ceremonies being a kind of act of consecration which gave a mystical sense of purpose to their 'community'. The midwinter festival of Yuletide was consciously intended to replace Christmas. An SS manual described it as the

> *greatest festival of our forebears. They advanced towards the Yule-night with firebrands to liberate the sun from bondage of wintry death and thought of it as a young hero come to rouse and free them from their death-like sleep. On Christmas Eve the main ingredients of festive fare must be carp, roast goose and wild boar – drawn respectively from the sphere of water, air and earth. In view of the fact that this is the greatest clan festival – it is becoming customary to exchange ideas about the success of the steadily deepening research into family genealogy.*

THE ELITE NATURE OF THOSE WHO VISITED THE CASTLE

Those who went to Wewelsburg were no longer bound by ordinary human ties but had their own loyalty to the brotherhood, an all-consuming passion to serve it and to cherish and follow its ideals. Wewelsburg was the cathedral where the senior 'priests' of Himmler's dark religion came to engage in their worship and be indoctrinated more deeply into the mythological universe he inhabited. They attempted to achieve a state of 'rapture' in which they could communicate with the Secret Chiefs, of whose wisdom they believed themselves to be the guardians.

This was far more than simply a feeling of privilege; it led to a feeling of exaltation that remained with them even after they had passed out of the immediate ambience of the castle. Even at the lower level of the SS, the preoccupation with doctrine, ritual and the search for this mystical sense of a higher purpose drove them on and not only enabled them to endure the hardships of the Russian Front to a greater extent than the regular troops but also to become hardened to the suffering of others.

The men who came to Wewelsburg and shared in the rites and ceremonies with Himmler were true believers. Their mission was to establish what they saw as an earthly paradise. They were utopians who truly believed that they were part of bringing about a new world where an aristocracy of racial supermen would rule and bring the perfect society into being.

The individual was seen as possessing no intrinsic worth; only as a part of the whole in an organic society was he capable of achieving value. It was the duty of the men who gathered at Wewelsburg, the SS generally and ultimately every human being, to renounce their individual personalities and subsume them within the task of becoming one of the 'new men' that it was the final objective of all their training to produce.

ROSENBERG AND LECTURES AT THE CASTLE

Rosenberg provided a number of lecturers to give talks at Wewelsburg. Some of them were on ordinary subjects such as politics, foreign policy, art and culture, prehistory, racial theory, philosophy and mysticism as well as more esoteric subjects. Some of the more exotic topics dealt with were symbolism; runes; mythology; alternative medicine; and the idea of 'eternal return', which was not simply a belief in individual reincarnation but also in the notion that the patterns of history itself recurred and that nations repeated an endless cycle of 'death and rebirth'. That particular theory was woven out of whole cloth by the Freiherr Stromer von Reichenbach, who essentially stole his ideas from the German philosophers Friedrich Nietzsche and Oswald Spengler as well as borrowing heavily from Hindu religion. Stromer's 'work' was described by one of Himmler's 'experts' as 'a new expression of the truly Nordic theory of the eternal return'. He also cultivated a reputation as a prophet and was one of Himmler's most influential 'intellectual' influences.

Although Stromer was an important influence on Himmler, particularly in terms of his growing obsession with Wewelsburg, Wiligut was his chief 'adviser' on occult matters. At Wiligut's suggestion Himmler added to the existing design plans the requirement to install a planetarium in the castle, no doubt to enable him to further his astrological interests and draw up predictions about the future of Germany and his own destiny. In addition he requested that the castle as the headquarters of an order of chivalry also needed a strong room to hold the 'treasure' he planned to place within it. Neither project was ever completed as the necessities of the war prevented the vast expenditure upon Wewelsburg of which Himmler and Wiligut had dreamed.

HIMMLER ANNOUNCES THE FINAL SOLUTION IN WEWELSBURG

In 1941 the castle served a more sinister purpose as Himmler convened a conference in March attended by Heydrich and various senior Nazi ministers and military leaders. At that conference he announced that Germany would be invading the Soviet Union in the near future and that not only would the invading forces be required to smash Communism but they would also be ordered to reduce the native population by thirty million. He also declared that Russian food supplies must be diverted to the service of the Reich and that Jews were among the highest priority targets to be eliminated in order to make way for the envisaged German settlers. Although he did not quite spell out the Final Solution in detail (that came later) there was no mistaking the sinister intention behind his speech. Not a word of protest came from the men seated around the table at Wewelsburg.

Himmler preached to his disciples at the castle and engaged in long sessions of silent meditation during which they all tried to make contact with and strengthen their ties with the 'Race Soul'. He instilled in them all the sense of a greater common purpose than that of the individual: the achievement of the triumph of the Aryan race and in particular the Germans over the 'lesser breeds'. Himmler demanded from them a blind obedience to orders, an inner hardness, strength of purpose and a commitment to bring about the imminent arrival of the 'New Man'. He saw Jews, Freemasons, Christians and Communists as all representing in different ways the opposite approach to his dark vision. Where he placed his faith was in the power of his new religion to transform the world. Communists and many Freemasons were either atheists or at least wedded to a view that happiness on earth was achievable. The Jews and Christians he saw as being governed by their fixation upon the individual. To Himmler the destiny of a single person was unimportant; it was the survival of the values of the group that mattered. As he once remarked in an extraordinary conversation with his masseur:

A man has to sacrifice himself, even though it is often very hard for him; he oughtn't to think of himself. Of course it's pleasanter to concern yourself with flower-beds rather than political dust-heaps and refuse-

dumps, but flowers themselves won't thrive unless these things are seen to. I try to help people and do good, relieve the oppressed and remove injustices wherever I can.

Bizarre though this outburst appears, Himmler made an even more extraordinary statement to his SS officers on 4 October 1943:

It is absolutely wrong to project your own harmless soul with its deep feelings, our kindheartedness, our idealism, upon alien peoples. One principle must be absolute for the SS man: we must be honest, decent, loyal, and comradely to members of our own blood and to no one else. What happens to the Russians, what happens to the Czechs, is a matter of utter indifference to me. Whether the other peoples live in comfort or perish of hunger interests me only in so far as we need them as slaves for our culture; apart from that it does not interest me. Whether or not 100,000 Russian women collapse from exhaustion while digging a tank ditch interests me only in so far as the tank ditch is completed for Germany. We Germans, who are the only people in the world who have a decent attitude to animals, will also adopt a decent attitude to these human animals, but it is a crime against our own blood to worry about them and to bring them ideals.

He goes on to say, speaking of what he frankly describes as 'the extermination of the Jewish people', in a tone of manifest admiration:

Most of you know what it means to see a hundred corpses lying together, five hundred, or a thousand. To have gone through this and yet to have remained decent, this has made us hard.

Such were the 'ideals' impressed upon the SS leaders who visited Wewelsburg and imbibed this distorted vision of 'decency', 'kindheartedness' and 'chivalry'.

THE END OF WEWELSBURG

Although work on the reconstruction of Wewelsburg continued until 1943 it came to an abrupt end that year. The pressing needs of Germany's military meant that funds could no longer be diverted to Himmler's grandiose project.

By that date only the North Tower of the castle had been completed. Eternally optimistic and dwelling in dreams that somehow victory for the Germans was still possible, Himmler chose to regard the end of work on Wewelsburg as a suspension rather than the termination of his project.

In February 1944 he wrote to the commandant in charge of the castle informing him of how often his thoughts turned towards Wewelsburg and how he planned to resume work on the project at the end of the war.

By March 1945 even Himmler realized that the war was lost. That month saw Allied forces surrounding Wewelsburg. Himmler became consumed with the desire that his castle of dreams should not fall into enemy hands. Rather than hand it over to the Allies he preferred to destroy it.

A team of SS commandos was sent to Wewelsburg to blow up the castle. On Easter Sunday 31 March 1945 they planted explosives and succeeded in destroying most of the building. Only the North Tower survived almost undamaged which immediately led to wild speculation about its possible 'magical powers'.

On 2 April 1945 the Americans captured Wewelsburg. They were initially baffled by the importance that Himmler attached to the castle but as members of the SS began to reveal their secrets its true significance finally became clear.

In 1949 work on rebuilding the castle began, the task of reconstruction continuing until 1979. It has since re-opened as a tourist attraction, housing a youth hostel and a museum. In 2010 the former SS guardhouse was converted into an exhibition centre describing life at Wewelsburg during the eleven years that it became the focal point of Himmler's occult fantasies.

Photographs, SS regalia and Himmler's teapot with runic inscriptions upon it are among the items showing how he tried to exemplify his dark vision through the castle. Wewelsburg shows most completely how far removed from everyday reality the world of the Nazi leadership really was and the extent to which their dreams were built upon occult and magical thinking.

Chapter Six
OCCULT REICH

IT WOULD NOT BE true to describe Nazi Germany as a state
primarily governed on occult principles. On the other hand it is equally
untrue to ignore, dismiss or downplay the extent to which such ideas
did play an important part in some areas of life, sometimes involving
key political, social and even military decisions.

IMPORTANCE OF OCCULT IDEAS IN THE EARLY YEARS OF NAZISM

The early twentieth century saw Germany awash with a range of mystical and occult ideas, a tendency that increased sharply after the nation's defeat in the First World War. Hitler's involvement with aspects of the occult dated back to his years as a drifter in Vienna, and when he joined the German Workers' Party he was actually becoming part of a magical order. The men he met through the small group that he turned into the Nazi Party were all steeped in occultism – Eckart, Rosenberg, Harrer, Feder and many others. It was the Thule Group leader Sebottendorf who founded what was to become the Party newspaper and who also took over what was to become the Nazi publishing house. Himmler and Hess were involved in almost every conceivable occult activity and seemed to believe virtually anything which was rejected by conventional science. Goering believed that the earth was hollow and that humans lived on the inside of it. Research into Atlantis and mythology attracted large amounts of government money even during the Second World War. Both Hitler and Goebbels were sufficiently skilled in astrology to be able to compare and interpret horoscopes themselves. The German Navy wasted huge sums of money on 'map dowsers' to try and identify the position of British ships.

The examples could go on almost indefinitely and what they point to is not a country where occultism ruled as such but one where 'magical' thinking permeated every level of the Party and influenced all aspects of life. It may be an exaggeration to suggest that Nazi Germany was dominated by the occult but certainly no nation since at least the eighteenth century had been so receptive to and so influenced by irrational ideas.

It was no accident that Hitler's appointment as Chancellor led not only to predictable attacks on Jews, Communists, socialists and liberals but also to a perhaps less expected campaign against occultism. There were a variety of reasons for this attack, some personal and others ideological. One was a desire to control every aspect of life within

Germany even in such peripheral areas as astrology and the occult. The other was a genuine fear of the supposed power of these fields.

In September 1919 Hitler met a Munich physician called Dr Wilhelm Gutberlet who remained friendly with him until his death. As Schellenberg put it: 'Hitler availed himself of Gutberlet's mystic power and had many discussions with him on racial questions.' Gutberlet believed that through using 'the sidereal pendulum' he was able to 'detect' Jews or people who simply possessed some Jewish ancestors. He was also a keen astrologer and may have helped to develop Hitler's skill at interpreting horoscopes. Sebottendorf was also an astrologer and wrote several books on the subject as well as editing a magazine. He also asked the question 'whether the Germans especially must give to the world a new species?'.

HANUSSEN – HITLER'S CLAIRVOYANT

One of the most influential occult practitioners throughout the 1920s and 1930s was an astrologer, fortune teller, clairvoyant and vaudeville entertainer who went under the professional name of Erik Jan Hanussen, although his real name was Herschel Steinschneider. At various periods of his life he worked as a stable boy, folk singer, trapeze artist and lion tamer as well as enjoying a brief spell as an opera singer. He had a sideline in blackmailing people to supplement his resources when times were hard.

After completing his military service he added hypnotism, telepathy, dowsing and stage magic to his list of accomplishments. Hanussen also belonged to an astrological group in Munich and some of its members were in regular contact with Hitler. He wrote two books, one before the First World War called *The Road to Telepathy: Explanation and Practice*. After the war he published another book known as *Thought Reading: A Primer for Telepathy*. In addition to his writing he was a master of creating atmosphere among the members of an audience, manipulating their expectations and using physical and psychological deception to impress them.

Hitler's favourite clairvoyant Erik Jan Hanussen with a client – when times were hard, he ran a sideline in blackmail.

Through the astrological group Hanussen met Hitler and immediately attracted the Nazi leader's attention by telling him he could improve his skill as a public speaker. Instead of being offended Hitler was interested and asked Hanussen to train him. He showed Hitler how to use gesture and body language as well as simply his voice to create a greater impact upon the audience. The effects were undeniable and soon Hanussen not only joined the Nazi Party but became a close confidant of Hitler.

Hanussen proceeded to exert himself to secure the victory of the Nazis. His own newspaper was edged with swastikas and full of astrological predictions of good fortune for the Party and its leader. Hanussen set up a Palace of Occultism where he gave public séances that were attended by many prominent Nazis.

On 26 February 1933 he made his most famous prediction. He announced that the Reichstag would be engulfed in flames and the very next day the building was on fire. The Reichstag fire still arouses controversy and even today there is no agreement among historians over what really happened or who was responsible for the conflagration. The three main theories in the field are that the Nazis started the fire themselves, that the Communists started the fire or that it was the work of a lone arsonist. There is actually far more reason to suspect the Communists of setting the blaze than is generally realized and the Nazis were certainly capable of anything; but the overwhelming balance of probability, supported by the testimony of independent and anti-Nazi eyewitnesses, is that the fire was the work of a single person. Marinus van der Lubbe was a serial arsonist who had already tried to burn down other buildings the same day. He was observed by anti-Nazi witnesses entering the building with incendiary material and even the police believed that he had acted alone.

Hanussen's prediction was one of the main reasons why people jumped to the conclusion that the Nazis must have been responsible. More baffling is the question as to why Hanussen ever had anything to do with the Nazi Party, let alone advising Hitler and working to secure his victory. He was Jewish and could hardly have been unaware of the anti-Semitism that stood at the very heart of Nazi thinking.

Whatever his reasons they did him no good. Six weeks after the Reichstag fire he was kidnapped, murdered and his body dumped in the woods near Berlin. He was not killed because of any 'secret knowledge' about Nazi plans although of course conspiracy theorists have put forward that suggestion. The truth is rather more prosaic and sordid. He had lent money to an SA leader who preferred to murder him rather than repay his debt.

Even allowing for the extent to which Hanussen and others helped develop the presentational side of Hitler's public performances his dramatic success was far more than simply the result of technical virtuosity. Hitler had an instinctive ability to influence people not only through his public speaking but even at close quarters and in private.

HITLER AND CROWDS

The relationship between Hitler and a crowd was a complex and unusual one. Hitler undoubtedly considered himself a great orator but his speeches appear to a later generation to be empty of content, delivered in a harsh and occasionally stammering voice and on the face of it unlikely to impress anyone who was not already a disciple. There is no doubt that millions of people even in Germany remained entirely immune to his powers of persuasion. On the other hand neutrals and even opponents admitted that when they heard Hitler speak it affected them profoundly and drew them at least momentarily into becoming part of his dark vision.

Hitler possessed the power to induce a state of ecstasy within a crowd. His effect was equally marked on men and women, old and young. William Shirer, author of *The Rise and Fall of the Third Reich*, described a Nazi rally in 1934. He was irresistibly reminded of the Holy Rollers, a religious sect whose members rolled around in ecstasy for hours, and he noted that the women in the audience gazed at Hitler in a state almost of sexual arousal. An anti-Nazi Englishman who spoke no German found himself at a rally where Hitler was speaking. To his amazement he found himself shouting 'Heil Hitler' with the rest of the audience and giving the Nazi salute.

Goebbels heard Hitler speak in Munich in June 1922 and was so captivated that he wrote to the Nazi leader declaring: 'You expressed more than your own pain. . . You named the need of a whole generation, searching in confused longing for men and tasks.'

The British Christian Ernestine Buller described a Nuremberg rally she attended as follows:

I was sitting surrounded by thousands of SA men and as Hitler spoke I was most interested at the shouts and more often the muttered exclamations of the men around me, who were mainly workmen or lower-middle class types. 'He speaks for me, he speaks for me.' 'Ach Gott, he knows how I feel.' Many of these seemed lost to the world around them and were probably unaware of what they were saying.

Even as a teenager Hitler was fascinated by the power of words and the effect of mass meetings on people. In Vienna he watched spellbound as the Social Democrats used these tactics to win converts to their cause. He told his friend August Kubizek after they had attended a performance of Wagner's opera *Rienzi* that one day he would have the power to move crowds as Rienzi had done.

Hitler consciously worked on overcoming opposition within crowds by what he called an appeal to 'hidden forces'. Particularly in his early years as Party leader, opposition from Communists, socialists and conservative nationalists was extremely common. His method of dealing with crowds, particularly hostile ones, was described vividly by Otto Strasser.

Hitler responds to the vibration of the human heart with the delicacy of a seismograph, or perhaps a radio-receiving set, enabling him, with a certainty with which no conscious gift could endow him, to act as a loudspeaker proclaiming the most secret desires, the least admissible instincts, the sufferings and personal revolts of a whole nation. Speaking as the spirit moves him, he is transformed into one of the greatest speakers of the century.

In essence what took place at these public meetings was a curious interaction of emotional energy between the speaker and the audience. Hitler was able to enter into the unconscious minds of those hearing him and somehow appeal to their fears, their need for reassurance, their dreams and longings and their desire for security and wholeness and was somehow able to persuade them on an entirely non-rational level that he held the key to providing them with inner peace. In a very real sense he activated the deep desire within millions of Germans for a Messiah to lead them into the Promised Land.

Hitler was in his element at a Nuremberg rally, when vast crowds were choreographed to demonstrate their subservience to his will and there was no chance of any heckling – the Führer *liked nothing better than to feel he was in control.*

HITLER AND PERSONAL MAGNETISM

It was not only upon crowds that Hitler was able to exert his influence. Even in small groups or on a one to one basis he possessed the power to convince people who were anything but weak-willed or hesitant to go along with his ideas. Men as powerful, self-confident and strong-willed as Goering, Goebbels, Himmler, von Blomberg and Schacht found themselves completely unable to withstand him. As Alan Bullock put it:

> *Until the last days of his life he retained an uncanny gift of personal magnetism which defies analysis but which many who met him have described. Hitler's power to bewitch an audience has been likened to the occult arts of the African medicine-man or the Asiatic shaman; others have compared it to the sensitivity of a medium and the magnetism of a hypnotist.*

What was the nature of this undoubted power over others? Was it mediumship, hypnotism or something else that enabled him to command others more gifted, more intelligent, more capable than himself and every bit as strong-willed?

Mediumship has often been suggested as an explanation but it does not really tally with how Hitler behaved or with its effect upon others. Mediums are essentially passive recipients of data, sensations and intuitions and no matter how attuned they may be to their audiences they do not produce the hysterical state of rapture that Hitler was able to evoke.

Hypnotism is a more plausible suggestion but even that is contradicted by both the physical and psychological effects that Hitler had on other people. A hypnotist puts his or her subject into a state of deep relaxation in order to make them more amenable to mental suggestion. No one ever felt relaxed in Hitler's presence either alone or among a crowd. That particular suggestion also fails to explain his power over others.

MESMERISM

Closely related to, but an entirely separate type of attempt to influence people, is the old-fashioned practice of mesmerism. This was founded by the Austrian doctor Franz Mesmer in the eighteenth century and was hugely popular for around a hundred years before falling out of favour in the latter part of the nineteenth century.

The patients of Mesmer and his disciples behaved in a remarkably different way from modern hypnotic subjects and also reported strikingly different physical symptoms. Far from becoming relaxed they appeared to go into a state of nervous excitement and even hysteria. The physical symptoms were also different, with patients reporting that feelings of extreme cold and heat often alternated with each other.

Curiously, both the physical and psychological effects of mesmerism resemble exactly those described by members of the audience at Hitler's public events and those who met with him in private. Mesmerism claimed to produce its effects through the agency of a force it described as 'animal magnetism'. From analysing the descriptions of this alleged form of energy it is clearly the same as the *vril* power that Hitler learned from the Vril Society in the early 1920s. Once again the extent to which occultism played a significant role in Hitler's life and the whole Nazi regime is demonstrated clearly.

ASTROLOGY AND THE NAZIS

An aspect of occultism that was to play a considerable part in the Nazi regime was astrology. The attitude towards it under the Nazis was always complex with Hitler, Himmler, Hess and others true believers and those like Goebbels and Bormann totally contemptuous. As the astrologer Gerda Walther, who was briefly arrested and interrogated by the Nazis in 1941, said, there was a 'complete lack of unity' on the subject of occult activities: 'Often there are different and even opposing points of view.'

What all the Nazis agreed upon whatever their attitude towards the credibility of astrology was that it needed to be brought firmly under the control of the government and could not be allowed to continue its independent existence. Some of the roots of this attitude developed out of the strange astrological civil war that took place in Germany during the 1920s and early 1930s.

THE ASTROLOGICAL CIVIL WAR

In 1923, a body designed to represent the interests of astrologers was formed, the Central Astrological Office (CAO). Almost immediately it was rocked by personality clashes and doctrinal disputes. The result was the formation of a rival organization in 1924, the Astrological Society in Germany (ASiG). Within the CAO the leading figures were Dr Hubert Korsch and Dr Wilhelm Mrsic. The main movers in the ASiG were Hugo Vollrath and Theobald Becher. There was an immediate and prolonged feud between Korsch and his rivals which was partly a battle of egos and partly genuine disagreement over the nature and future of astrology.

Korsch believed that astrology was a genuine science and needed to cleanse itself of its superstitious baggage and shake off its reputation as a dubious branch of fortune telling. Vollrath was a confidence trickster who had been expelled from the Theosophical Society and also had at least two aliases which he used to extract money from naive people in return for worthless 'diplomas'. He was exactly the sort of charlatan Korsch detested and Vollrath's additional tendency to utter pretentious claptrap at great length infuriated him. Becher was not personally disreputable but took the view that astrology should be allowed to continue on its traditional 'amateur' basis and that there was no real need to impose standards and testing procedures upon its practitioners.

Two factors complicated the position of astrology in Germany during this period. One was the emergence of a completely new 'system' known as the Hamburg School. This system was founded by Alfred Witte and was based on the idea that a planet beyond Neptune existed within the solar system. Witte's disciples were duly exultant at the discovery of Pluto in 1930. The other factor was of course the rise of Hitler's movement.

Astrologers were no more immune from the instability of their country than any other group within Germany. Many became directly involved in politics to a greater or lesser degree. Some were fiercely anti-Nazi while others became supporters. Probably the majority of pro-Nazi astrologers changed their orientation for practical reasons of self-interest and a desire for survival but many really did subscribe to the Nazi racial myths and were therefore compelled to evolve a 'Nordic' astrology to justify their beliefs.

ELSBETH EBERTIN'S HOROSCOPE FOR HITLER

Before turning to the Nordic astrologers and the consequences of the rise of Nazism upon their movement and on astrology in Germany generally, it is necessary to examine the career of the leading German practitioner Elsbeth Ebertin. She was already firmly established as one of the principal astrologers in Germany before a prediction that she gave in 1923 turned her overnight into the most famous exponent in the country, if not the world.

Ebertin was approached by a female supporter of the Nazis and asked to cast a horoscope for an unnamed individual and predict his future on the basis of his chart. Unfortunately the woman was unable to furnish Ebertin with the time of his birth so the astrologer employed a technique known as 'rectification' where various different charts are drawn up and the one that seems the likeliest fit with the client is selected. Her calculations were made during the spring of 1923 and published in July of the same year in her annual almanac *Ein Blick in die Zukunft* (A Glimpse into the Future). Ebertin's prediction was:

A man of action born on 20 April 1889, with sun in 29 degrees Aries at the time of his birth, can expose himself to personal danger by excessively uncautious action and could very likely trigger off an uncontrollable crisis. His constellations show that this man is to be taken very seriously indeed; he is destined to play a 'Führer role' in future battles. It seems that the man I have in mind, with this strong Aries movement, is destined to sacrifice himself for the German nation, also to face up to all circumstances with audacity and courage, even when it is a matter of life and death, and to give an impulse, which will burst forth quite suddenly, to a German Freedom movement.

Later that year the failed Munich Putsch took place. The result was to catapult Hitler from the leader of a fringe movement in Bavaria to national prominence and to establish him and the Nazis as a serious political party. It also did no harm to Ebertin's career as an astrologer.

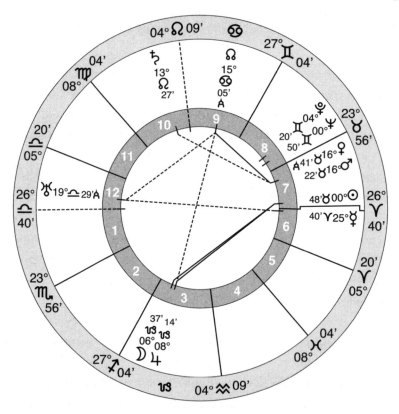

Hitler's birthchart – born 6.22 pm 20/4/1889: this is the horoscope of a man gifted at public expression, yet who finds it hard to listen to others.

In early 1924 she co-authored a book called *The Stars in their Courses and World Events* which sold 70,000 copies. It revealed that during the summer of 1923 she had sent a copy of her almanac to the *Völkischer Beobachter* and that Hitler had been made aware of her warning. She also discovered the correct time of Hitler's birth and so was able to draw up a more correct chart and interpretation of his destiny. Hitler later referred more than once to Ebertin's prediction and declared that it had helped boost his career. She was left unmolested throughout the Third Reich though the last edition of her almanac appeared in 1937.

NORDIC ASTROLOGY

The Nazi involvement in the astrological civil war began with the entry of a Party member called Martin Pfefferkorn. His first attempt to gain control of astrology was to set up an organization of his own known as the *Arbeitsgemeinschaft Deutscher Astrologen* (ADA) in 1932, which he claimed would reflect National Socialist activities. He tried to affiliate his group with the ASiG but was turned down by Vollrath and Becher. Hitler's appointment as Chancellor radically transformed both the political situation and Pfefferkorn's prospects. He aspired to become the *Führer* of German astrology and as a Nazi Party member he suddenly acquired weight and influence.

Korsch had founded an astrological magazine known as *Zenit* in 1930 which was far superior to any of its competitors in the field. Unfortunately for him an article by one of his contributors in November 1932 was considered politically incorrect by Pfefferkorn who promptly began a feud with Korsch.

Vollrath and Becher joined the Nazi Party to try and protect their own position. Seizing upon the chance to supplant Korsch's predominant position in German astrology they joined forces with Pfefferkorn. There followed an attempt to destroy Korsch and his CAO through suggestions that he was Jewish and that his political loyalties were suspect. Korsch was able to disprove the claims about his ancestry but as someone who had only joined the Nazis in May 1933 he was widely distrusted. It was ironic that Pfefferkorn's approach to astrology was closer to Korsch's than it was to charlatans like Vollrath.

On 12 June 1933 Pfefferkorn became the new president of the ASiG with Becher as his vice-president and Vollrath as a senior committee member. For the moment Pfefferkorn's dream of becoming the astrological *Führer* appeared close to being realized. Korsch was under suspicion and Pfefferkorn felt sure that his rival would soon be eliminated.

NAZI SUPPRESSION OF ASTROLOGY

The political wind began to change during the autumn of 1933. In spite of Pfefferkorn's new status, there was a growing desire among the higher echelons of the leadership to control or even suppress astrology altogether. There was an internal power struggle within the Party on the whole question as part of the ongoing process of *Gleichschaltung* – integration. On the one side stood those like Hess, Himmler and Rosenberg, who believed that astrology enshrined essential truths and only needed to be controlled and regulated in the service of the state. Against them stood Goering, Goebbels and Bormann who regarded the inherent 'universalism' of astrology as incompatible with National Socialist ideology and looked on all of its practitioners as potential enemies of the state.

Slowly but surely the second view became the dominant one within the Party. In the autumn of 1933 the process of suppression began when the police chiefs of Berlin, Hanover and Cologne issued a decree that all newspapers within their jurisdiction must refuse any advertisements by astrologers. The spring of 1934 saw the Berlin police issue a ban on all kinds of 'fortune telling' for money. This not only forbade astrologers from charging fees for their services but also made it illegal for them to sell almanacs and magazines.

By October 1934 Pfefferkorn ended his feud with Korsch and handed over in favour of Becher. He had realized that there was no future for a professional astrologer in Nazi Germany and concentrated instead on his Party activities. Korsch may have mistaken this signal and been emboldened by the new development but he certainly took advantage of it to launch an attack on Vollrath in December 1934. He showed that Vollrath had faked his doctorate and forged his dissertation.

All this grandstanding soon became inconsequential as the police began to enter bookshops and confiscate all astrological literature. This brought publishers, booksellers and authors into an unwelcome alliance with the astrologers against the authorities. At a conference on 27–8 October in Berlin an attempt was made to create a body that could negotiate directly with the authorities to protect the interests of all the threatened parties. Korsch opposed the plan and was assaulted by a rival astrologer. Eventually a committee was formed that negotiated with the authorities and a compromise solution was found.

Under the terms of the agreement a censorship office for astrological literature was set up under the leadership of Karl-Friedrich Schulze. Naturally Schulze was a Nazi but he was so diplomatic that even Korsch did not oppose his appointment. In July 1935 astrologers were incorporated into the German Labour Front as 'independent professionals' and came under the control of Schulze.

Now that the civil war among the astrologers was finally over a process of slow attrition was employed to wear them down. One by one their publications ceased and their activities went underground. Even before the open crackdown in 1941 independent astrologers had all but vanished from Germany. Only those who were tolerated (like Ebertin) or those like Wilhelm Wulff and Karl Krafft who were useful servants of the regime continued to practise their art in obscurity. Most of those who survived did so by working for Himmler's *Ahnenerbe*. Himmler explained the motivation behind the suppression as follows:

> *In the Third Reich we have to forbid astrology. We cannot permit any astrologers to follow their calling except those who are working for us. In the National Socialist state astrology must remain a privilegium singularum. It is not for the broad masses.*

It was not only astrology that was banned or harnessed to the service of the state. All occult organizations soon found themselves being suppressed. Even pro-Nazi ones like the Thule Group, the Vril Society, Lanz's New Templars and the Germanen Order fell foul of the ban and were forbidden to operate. This decision was not taken out of a rationalist desire to combat superstition but from fear of the 'power' that the Nazis believed occultism to possess. That is why dowsers, astrologers, clairvoyants, mediums and numerologists soon found themselves working for the Nazis in spite of their official suppression. Himmler was so obsessed with astrology that Heydrich remarked sarcastically that: 'Goering is worried about the stars on his chest [his medals], Himmler about the stars in his horoscope.'

RUNES

As well as astrology, runes were another obsession with Himmler's *Ahnenerbe*, but people's interest in them long predated the Nazi era. The first suggestion that they possessed magical properties was made by the Roman historian Tacitus in the first century AD. He described the Teutonic tribes using marks carved on tree branches as a means of foretelling the future. The ancient Viking sagas also relate how spells were chanted over runic symbols carved on wood. In the eighteenth century runes became a fashionable interest among German, Scandinavian and British writers and antiquarians. By the nineteenth century they had become assimilated into German *völkisch* thought.

Guido von List first fashioned the generalized respect for runes into a systematic way of interpreting the past in a new light. Even he described his work as 'archaeological occultism' and it certainly provided a highly idiosyncratic use for an interpretation of runic inscriptions. Ancient burial mounds, coats of arms, *völkisch* art, symbols in churches, patterns in the landscape and the sign of the swastika were among the areas he researched and as a result he claimed to have discovered the secret sacred language of the Aryan religious leaders.

The Karlevi Runestone, Öland, Sweden, complete with its verse to a proud Nordic warrior fallen in battle who lies buried in the mound below.

Von List believed that the secret meaning of the runes was concealed in a hidden code contained within the stained glass windows of Gothic churches. By deciphering the code it was possible to unlock the mysteries of alchemy. Clues to the mystical significance of the runes could also be found in the writings of Meister Eckhart, Paracelsus and Jakob Boehme, with runic divination making it possible to decode their hidden meaning.

Von List also believed that words had power in themselves and provided the connecting link between the material world and the world of thought. Certain words of power could bring about changes on the physical plane if they were uttered correctly. The alphabet itself came from prehistoric humanity's study of the heavens and each letter was somehow related to a particular star or planet. The sun and moon were the principal movers of human destiny and the ultimate sources of language and the alphabet.

Von List made much of the fact that the Gothic word *runa* – the earliest form of the word 'rune' – means 'secret'. He also claimed that the Kabbalah was not a form of Jewish mysticism but had originated among the Visigothic Germans in Spain. The theory about an association between runes and the Kabbalah was first proposed in the seventeenth century by Johannes Bureus.

In 1908 von List published a set of eighteen symbols which he described as 'Armanen runes'. Later Wiligut created another set of runes that were partly derived from von List's. Wiligut designed the SS-*Ehrenring* which included several of his own runic symbols. From 1933 onwards Himmler added the Sig runes to SS insignia.

THE NAZIS AND LEY LINES

Another aspect of the occult that fascinated many Nazis was the idea of ley lines. Himmler was the most enthusiastic senior Nazi on the subject and laid out Wewelsburg in accordance with its principles. The theory of leys was created originally by a British writer named Alfred Watkins but soon found many disciples in Germany. Its leading German exponent was Dr Josef Heinsch.

Heinsch adopted Watkins' theory of ley lines but radically transformed it. Unlike the British writer he did not believe that leys were ancient roads and saw them instead as an early form of town planning with sacred sites providing the focus around which the ley lines were created. Heinsch claimed that there was an exact correspondence between the patterns on prehistoric landscapes and the proportions of buildings and monuments found in sacred sites. According to Heinsch stone circles, pagan temples and Christian churches all demonstrated the same numerical relationship.

Heinsch declared that prehistoric people employed the metre as their unit of measurement when calculating the leys and the sacred sites with which they were connected. In his view the choice of this unit was 'cosmically defined' by its status as 'a ten-millionth of the Earth's quadrant'. He made no attempt to explain how it is that other units of measurement have been found among prehistoric people or how it was that the 'Imperial' system of measuring was a more common choice of unit.

Heinsch gave examples ranging from Stonehenge, Solomon's Temple, Notre Dame and the Temple of Amun at Karnak in Egypt. He believed that the number 42 possessed some kind of cosmic significance which led to its employment as an aspect of what he called 'sacred geometry'. He claimed that Notre Dame, a Sumerian temple and a stone circle at Odry in Czechoslovakia all exemplified the factor of 42. Heinsch pointed out that in the *Grímnismál*, a poem within the Norse *Eddas*, there was 'a 42-stage ascent and re-ascent from the heavenly to the earthly'. He went on to claim that the principles of 'sacred geometry' led to the development of 'sacred engineering' before digressing into ramblings about the *Vehm* (spelt *Veme* by Heinsch) and dragging in various festivals and folk customs. Speculations on place names and the etymological roots of various German words followed.

Heinsch did not confine himself to abstract thinking but was able to put his ideas into practice. Himmler's backing led to Heinsch becoming involved in 'a general housing plan, with its functional divisions into areas, provision for green-belts, transportation corridors, extension of the road system, etc., for the second largest of the German rural districts then undergoing industrial development'.

Himmler adopted Heinsch's theories and attempted to make them the basis of architecture and civil engineering throughout Germany. Speer had different ideas and as a professional architect was more successful in seeing his visions realized. All the same 'sacred geometry' and 'sacred engineering' were projects on which Himmler's *Ahnenerbe* spent considerable time and money.

During the course of their researches they decided that there was a relationship between the earth's magnetic radiation and the 'sacred measurements' used by prehistoric people. The war made it impossible for this theory to be worked out fully but it became the basis of the later theories of 'telluric forces' and 'earth energies'.

SYMBOLISM

Symbolism more generally played a huge part in Nazi thought and propaganda. As well as the swastika, the 'death's-head' symbol was particularly associated with the SS and of course had its own macabre and chilling effect on those who viewed it. Even the Iron Cross had double-edged overtones with the Cross – an ancient symbol of Christianity – associated with war rather than peace. Rosenberg also tried to associate the symbolism of the sword with the Nazi regime in a conscious attempt to assimilate its medieval and chivalric connotations with the National Socialist philosophy of life. He wanted a sword to be laid on the altar of every church in Germany and placed alongside *Mein Kampf.*

The members of the Armanen Society introduced the 'heil' greeting which they took from ancient Teutonic pagan custom. Von List claimed that the swastika was 'the holiest symbol' of his mythical ancient Armanen priesthood. The Thule Group also adopted the swastika as their symbol of choice. Sebottendorf declared that it was the rune of

Walvater (the All-Father) and represented the sun, the element of fire, the eagle and of course the Aryan race. Lanz also chose the swastika as the symbol for his New Templar Order.

The swastika was regarded as both a symbol of the sun and of the life force, the *vril* power. It was believed to have electromagnetic properties and at the annual solstice ceremonies the sun was imagined to bestow occult wisdom as well as its more obvious physical effects. Von List declared that it held the key to what he called 'secret science' and had the power to strengthen German blood and develop the facility of clairvoyance. According to von List the human race originated on the moon and the swastika was 'one of the holiest secret signs'.

Although the swastika is a very ancient symbol of the sun that has been used by people all over the world since prehistoric times a *völkisch* author named Ernst Krause appears to have been the first to claim in his book *Twiskoland*, published in 1891, that it was a specifically Aryan symbol. Ungern-Sternberg used it on the stamps of his brief Mongolian empire. Rosenberg claimed that it was an 'ancestral memory' of an Arctic sun.

THE NEW MAN – THE NEXT STAGE IN HUMAN EVOLUTION

There was considerable activity within the occult field in Nazi Germany, even if most of it did take place underground. Himmler actually remarked that 'science' would soon be replaced by *'geheimwissenschaft'* – 'occult science'. The ultimate goal of the illuminated National Socialists went far beyond the simple military and political domination of the world. In the same way their obsession with the creation of an Aryan Master Race went far beyond simple racism and into areas that read like the imaginings of a science fiction novelist.

The whole focus of the occult aspects of Nazism was geared towards realizing what they saw as the next stage of human evolution and the creation of the 'New Man' who would be as far above the Aryans as in their eyes they were already above all other humans. Hitler and Himmler worked tirelessly towards achieving the triumph of the 'New Man' to a greater degree than any other Nazi leaders. As Hitler said:

> *Creation is not yet completed. All creative forces will be concentrated on a new species. The two types of man, the old and the new, will evolve rapidly in different directions. One will disappear from the face of the Earth, the other will flourish. This is the real motive behind the National Socialist movement.*

Hitler also claimed that: 'Man is becoming God – that is the simple fact. Man is God in the making.' All the various occult techniques that Himmler in particular employed created

> *a fanatical autohypnosis which convinced disciples, succumbing to the totalitarian discipline in the promise of reaching a transcendent reality, that they were the new men the age was waiting for, that they were endowed with a secret energy which would enable them to take over Germany and the world.*

The 'New Man' visualized by Hitler had developed his psychic powers to their fullest extent. He would not only be physically stronger and intellectually superior but his psychic and spiritual development would raise him to the level of a divine being. The New Man would have mastered the secrets of time travel and be able to visit the distant past and the remote future with equal ease. He would possess an enhanced imagination that allowed him to perceive and understand everything instantly without the need for rational thought or a careful evaluation of facts. His 'superclairvoyance' would enable him to see everything and know the innermost thoughts of everyone. The power of 'magical speech' was given to him and this power would enable him to control all lesser beings. Other humans, even spirits, the weather and the atoms of the universe would all be subject to his controlling will. These 'new men' were described by Hitler as 'the final state in human mutation – the Man God!'

As well as all of these powers, the New Man would also be physically different from existing humans. He would be a giant in size and strength and his pineal gland would be so highly developed that it would be visible as a literal third eye. Hitler referred to it as the 'Cyclops eye' and declared:

A new age of magic interpretation of the world is coming, of interpretation in terms of the will and not the intelligence. There is no such thing as truth, either in the moral or in the scientific sense. The New Man would be the antithesis of the Jew.

A similarly bizarre remark was made by Hitler in his *Table Talk* where he declared: 'I imagine to myself that one day science will discover in the waves set in motion by the Rheingold secret mutual relations connected with the order of the world.'

Every aspect of the Nazi endeavour was ultimately dedicated to the realization of this dark vision. Himmler's programmes of selective breeding were designed to achieve it on the biological level just as his training programme for the SS attempted to bring it about on a psychological and spiritual plane. On a wider scale a variety of other methods were employed to hasten the arrival of this next step in evolution in which the Nazi inner circle believed. The obsession with racial purity and the superiority of the Nordic German variety of human being was relentlessly drummed into the heads of Germans just as the inferior and 'subhuman' status of other ethnic types was fashioned into a hypnotic hymn of hatred. The compulsory sterilization of 'inferior racial types' and the compulsory euthanasia of mental patients all aimed at 'improving' the 'stock' of the German people even through murder and brutality. The Final Solution which saw the deliberate extermination on purely racial grounds of Jews and gypsies was also implemented with the same objectives in mind.

Behind the facade of rationalism and the calculated use of modern technology to provide the driving force for the regime lay this twisted vision of a race of superhuman beings. It was in order to bring about a world in which such life forms could dominate the remainder of the human race that Hitler, Himmler and other leading Nazis sacrificed the lives of millions.

These ideas strike us now as the ravings of a madman or the dark imagination of a writer of horror stories. They were of course fantasies and mercifully never came close to being realized. The fact that they were crazy, impractical and repellent did not mean that Hitler and his inner circle did not genuinely seek to bring them about or that they believed them to be unrealistic. On the contrary, they strove to achieve them precisely because they genuinely thought they were both desirable and possible.

The great tragedy is that for twelve years the people who believed in these ideas had the power to put them into practice and as a result to bring about the needless death of millions of other human beings. An almost equal tragedy is that so many Germans welcomed their utter dehumanization at the hands of the Nazis. As one expressed it in the 1930s, 'we Germans are so happy. We are free of freedom'. A sad epitaph indeed for a regime that promised its people so much and delivered so little.

Chapter Seven

IN SEARCH OF ATLANTIS

THE STORY OF ATLANTIS was first written down by Plato in the fourth century BC and it immediately captured the imagination of the world. He described an essentially Bronze Age civilization that allegedly lay beyond the Pillars of Heracles – the Greek name for the Straits of Gibraltar – and was a mighty empire that dominated the world until it was overthrown by a combination of Greek warriors defending their homeland and a cosmic catastrophe that sounded very much like an earthquake. According to Plato the island continent sank beneath the ground and was never seen again.

There has always been fierce debate over whether Plato's 'lost continent of Atlantis' ever existed at all and there is still more disagreement over its location among those who accept that his account was based on memories of a real sunken land. A bewildering variety of places have been suggested as the 'true' site of Atlantis and to this day no unequivocal conclusion has been reached by researchers in the field. Broadly speaking the theories fall into three main categories. One school accepts Plato's account as literally true and therefore believes that an advanced civilization existed somewhere in the region of the Atlantic. Another group believes that Plato's story was based on real events but that his dates and geography are mistaken and the 'true' Atlantis flourished some nine thousand years later than he said and was a far smaller and less important land than he presents it as being. The third view is that Plato's story is true in essentials but is a composite of several mythical and legendary sources which he conflated into a single myth. This third view is probably the correct explanation of the Atlantis story.

Whatever the reality there is no doubt that the Germans were fascinated by the legend of Atlantis long before the Nazis came to power. It is also beyond dispute that at no time in human history did any government spend as much money and effort upon researching the story as the Nazis devoted to the lost land.

Himmler and Rosenberg were particularly interested in providing the truth of the story even though they associated it with a northern land. In their eyes the lost Atlantis existed either in the region of the Arctic or somewhere in the North Atlantic, in the vicinity of Iceland and Greenland. The majority of German research into Atlantis was founded by Himmler's *Ahnenerbe*.

THE GERMAN OBSESSION WITH ESTABLISHING AN EXALTED PREHISTORY

The Nazi desire to establish a more exalted origin for the German people and the wish to identify them with an antiquity greater than

Greece, Rome or even Egypt led to an obsession with an Atlantean origin for the Aryan race.

Even among the Nazis there were numerous ideas about the 'true' location of Atlantis. Throughout the 1920s a number of German 'experts' on the subject published books that all suggested a different site for the 'real' Atlantis. Some of them at least attempted to be scholarly while others were clearly written by people with at best a minimal grasp on reality.

Olof Rudbeck claimed in 1675 that Atlantis lay in Sweden and that all subsequent civilization derived from a Swedish source. He called his Atlantis Atland and declared that it was the 'Manheim' – the original home of mankind. Rudbeck believed that Scandinavia was the first part of Europe to be colonized by survivors from Atlantis. These early Scandinavians brought civilization to the less advanced people throughout Europe. He also declared that Swedish was the original language of mankind and had been spoken by Adam and Eve.

The eighteenth-century French writer Jean-Sylvain Bailly became converted to Rudbeck's views and suggested that the remnants of Atlantis could be found on the island of Spitsbergen in Norway. In the nineteenth century, Rudbeck's notion of Atland was taken up but identified with yet another 'lost land' that was not the same as Plato's Atlantis. Many Nazis were also attracted by Rudbeck's idea, including a man who for a while became a close adviser to Himmler and head of the *Ahnenerbe*, Hermann Wirth.

Atlantis has been 'found' on numerous occasions and in 1926 the German geologist Paul Borchardt declared that he had 'discovered' it in Algeria and Tunisia. Albert Hermann, a German archaeologist and geographer, explored Tunisia and announced that he had 'found' the site of Atlantis. Hermann appears to have been the first Atlantologist – people who study the problem of Atlantis – to suggest that Plato's dates and measurements were out by a factor of ten. He claimed that the destruction of Atlantis really took place around 1400BC rather than nine thousand years earlier and that it involved a much smaller land mass than that described in Plato's account. Hermann also declared that his Tunisian Atlantis was only a 'colony' of a great German civilization based around Friesland, which had dominated Western Europe and built Stonehenge. Its 'colony' in Tunisia was the beginning of 'Mediterranean civilization'.

Adolf Schulten proposed a different location for 'his' Atlantis. He believed that it lay on the Guadalquivir estuary in Spain and corresponded with the ancient Phoenician colony of Tartessos or Tartessus. Schulten also declared that this Spanish Atlantis was a 'colony' of the German civilization that had dominated Western Europe at the time.

Leo Frobenius claimed to have 'discovered' Atlantis in Nigeria and he associated it with German sources. The swastika and various other

'How I Found the Lost Atlantis' was the headline that went with this map in the London Budget, *a now-defunct newspaper, in 1931. Mankind has long been obsessed with Atlantis, but the Nazis turned it into an ideological goldmine.*

völkisch symbols were traced back by him to this region and offered as evidence of a German connection with Atlantis.

All of these writers made exaggerated claims and were obsessed with the idea of somehow fitting the legend of Atlantis into their notions of German superiority. They did at least attempt to rest their theories upon some degree of evidence and tried to argue in favour of them rationally. With the Atlantologists whose views found most favour with the Nazis it was an entirely different story.

VÖLKISCH THEORIES OF ATLANTIS

Wirth was chosen by Himmler as the original head and prime mover of the activities of the *Ahnenerbe*. He claimed that Atlantis lay in the region of the North Pole and had spread out from its Arctic homeland to colonize and bring civilization to the rest of the world. The Atlanteans not only settled in Europe, he said, but travelled as far afield as Polynesia. Wirth claimed that the Atlanteans were a 'Nordic' people who spread 'Germanic' culture across the world.

He combined pseudo-history with the worst excesses of occult fantasies and believed that 'the original Aryan civilization' came from his polar Atlantis and incorporated the idea of an 'eternal recurrence'. Wirth also wrote extensively on 'Atlantean symbolism' and his disciple Alfred Bäumler declared that 'to whomever perceived this trail there appears a new dimension of reality'.

Wirth's combination of surface learning with Aryan fantasies soon brought him to the attention of Himmler. As well as his cranky ideas on prehistory Wirth also displayed a considerable degree of personal oddity. He was a vegetarian who was firmly convinced that his wife was a gifted clairvoyant. Visitors to his home were greeted by a sign reading 'Please walk softly and do not smoke; a deep breather lives here'. The 'deep breather' was his wife and (at least in public) she hardly ever spoke. Guests observed her sitting in silence with a golden fillet around her brow. Wirth then read her thoughts telepathically as she breathed deeply and 'interpreted' them to his visitors.

Wirth was placed in charge of the *Ahnenerbe* expedition to Bohuslän in Sweden. He studied the stone engravings he found there and interpreted most of them as symbols of an 'Arctic sun'. Wirth declared that the idea of a resurrected god came from the long periods of northern darkness and their eventual replacement by a period when light was prevalent.

ATLAND

In addition to his idea of an Atlantis at the North Pole, Wirth also popularized the claims for the existence of yet another 'lost land'. Atland (a name used earlier by Rudbeck) was said to be a colony of Atlantis that had survived the destruction of its parent land and had spread civilization in its turn to the non-Nordic countries on earth. It was alleged to lie between Greenland and the Scottish Hebrides.

The idea of Atland was based on a nineteenth-century forgery called the *Oera Linda Book*. This work claimed that the great culture heroes

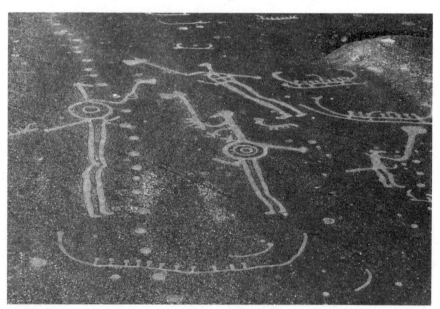

The Bohuslän petroglyphs in Sweden are the largest concentration of rock carvings in Scandinavia – Wirth credited the 'Arctic sun' as inspiration.

of Europe during the semi-mythical times of Crete, early Greece and other lands were actually 'Friesians'. These Friesians were the bringers of Teutonic civilization to the non-Nordics. In spite of its being an obvious forgery (not even Rosenberg believed in its authenticity), Himmler was firmly convinced that the work was 'an Aryan intellectual treasure'. When a German professor dared to publicly denounce it as a fake Himmler sent him a stern rebuke that terrified him into silence.

Wirth hated Christianity and spoke out against it constantly to such an extent that pro-Nazi Christians began to complain. Another source of conflict was Wirth's belief that the Aryan race had originally been a matriarchal rather than patriarchal society and that Germany should be attempting to put women in most of the positions of power. It was probably tactical reasons of retaining Christian support and making the Nazis appear more rational than they really were that led Hitler to condemn Wirth publicly at a Nuremberg Party rally in 1936. Himmler still regarded Wirth highly but realized he could no longer allow him to be the principal mover in the *Ahnenerbe*. He quietly eased Wirth out of positions of responsibility and made Wolfram Sievers the new head of his organization. Rosenberg also took advantage of the situation to denounce Wirth for what he described as his 'chthonic feminism' which he claimed was entirely incompatible with the 'patriarchal structure' of 'Aryan societies'.

RUDOLF STEINER AND ATLANTIS

Rudolf Steiner was always regarded as a mortal enemy by the Nazis but many of his ideas were sufficiently similar to theirs to become incorporated into their occult mythology. The source of the 'acceptable' aspects of Steiner's ideas was never credited but as there was considerable overlap between the views of many German occultists it was not hard to adopt an idea from one 'thinker' and assign its origin to another.

Steiner's account of Atlantis made no pretensions to being based upon history or archaeology. His occult fantasies were almost entirely derived from his 'highly developed clairvoyance'.

WRDEN MOSTE. MI SON OM. ER BY WIL
DON IA AT IARA SKRIT VNLESBER SHOL
WESA FAR ORA FOLKUM. WAND IA AVA
ALTID EMNESA. US TODVANDE SIND IA
ERDE FONA WIS RAKA. ER META AT A
BARN A SKRITTUN IARAR ALORUM AM.
PER LESA EN MWOA. DA WILI WI VSA
ALDER ALDESTA SKRITTUN EVIN RED LESA
MWOE AS ERA ER ISTER SKREVEN SIND.
AIF IS AT STAND SKRIT. ER VNDER AT RUN
SKRIT. FOR A ATAL. NOMAR A BIDER WISA

STAND.

RUN.

The Oera Linda Book *was supposed to have been compiled between* 2194BC *and*
AD803. *The fact it was a fake didn't stop it from being translated into several languages.*

According to Steiner the kings of Atlantis were instructed by what he called 'Messengers of the Gods'. There were also disciples who carried the teachings of the 'messengers' with them as they colonized Europe, Asia, Africa and America.

Steiner claimed that when Atlantis sank beneath the waves it also drained the Gobi Desert. As a result much of the lost wisdom of the continent found its way to Tibet where it was preserved. The survivors of Atlantis gradually transmitted their superior wisdom to the Aryans, who eventually produced their finest flowering in the Teutonic people.

According to Steiner the Atlanteans also possessed highly evolved psychic powers. They were able to communicate telepathically rather than through speech and could control natural forces through 'etheric technology'. He also claimed that the Aryans were descended from Atlantean survivors and were linked to 'present-day civilized humanity'. This statement shows clearly how much Steiner was influenced by *völkisch* thinking. It is no accident that Steiner tried to recruit Eckart as one of his disciples. Even though the two men fell out instead of co-operating, many of their ideas were not significantly different.

ATLANTIS AND TIBET

Throughout the 1920s reports of mysterious hidden civilizations in Mongolia or Tibet became more frequent. The Chinese doctor Lao-Tsin described a journey among the mountains of Tibet which led to his discovery of a secret valley where he claimed there was a 'tower of Shambhala' containing laboratories and many scientists. The doctor also observed demonstrations of telepathy across considerable distances.

The Lamas of Tibet claimed that 'northern Shambhala' was once an enormous ocean that contained an island. Then an event which sounds rather like a large meteorite or planetoid crashing down on earth led to its destruction so that only sand, salt lakes and mountains now remained of the former paradise.

One of Himmler's favourite anthropologists, Albert Grünwedel, translated a Tibetan book called *The Path to Shambhala*. Nicholas Roerich also made journeys to Tibet where he heard stories of subterranean kingdoms, secret wisdom and lost treasures from an immemorial antiquity.

ROSENBERG AND ATLANTIS

Rosenberg was as obsessed with Atlantis as Himmler and made it one of the key motifs of his *Myth of the 20th Century*. He used the book to declare that Atlantis was the original home of the Aryan race.

> *And those waves of Atlantean people travelled by water on their swan and dragon ships into the Mediterranean, to Africa; by land over central Asia to Kutschka, indeed, perhaps even to China, across north America to the south of the continent.*

Rosenberg was convinced that the 'true' location of Atlantis lay in the north of Europe. He explained such symbols as the swastika as being 'racial memories' of an Arctic sun. All non-Aryan races derived from a mixture of 'Atlantean blood' with that of other 'primitive peoples'.

Rosenberg's vision of Atlantis was part of an attempt by himself, Himmler and other Nazis to formulate a radically different view of world history. They saw the Atlantis myth as part of a mission to 'reclaim' what they regarded as a 'lost' German past. The reality was that they were inventing a mythical prehistory to glorify their ancestors and create the illusion that Germans had always been the prime movers in world civilization. The Germans had not been primitive barbarians but instead had led the world in bringing humanity out of its formerly backward condition. Rosenberg expressed his views as follows:

> *From a northern centre of creation which, without postulating an actual submerged Atlantic continent, we may call Atlantis, swarms of warriors once fanned out, in obedience to the ever-renewed and incarnate Nordic longing for distance to conquer and space to shape.*

Rosenberg claimed that his northern master race had originated in Atlantis and had been a warrior people dwelling in the north during prehistoric times when the climate was very different from what it was in his day. He claimed that the Atlanteans migrated as far east as Russia, Iran and India. His theories declared that the Germans were the purest descendants of the ancient Atlanteans and he threw together highly selective excerpts from the Hindu *Vedas* and the Zoroastrian *Zend-Avesta* to support his claims. In his opinion the Odinist pagan religion of pre-Christian Germany and Scandinavia also represented a survival of the original religion of the people of Atlantis.

Rosenberg's own occult institute was called Amt Rosenberg. It was always less well funded and influential than Himmler's *Ahnenerbe* but was also less prone to completely irrational ideas. Rosenberg saw world history as a continual struggle between the pure-blooded Germans who were the sole authentic survivors of Atlantis and their deadly enemies the Jews.

THE HOUSE OF ATLANTIS

A German who was an ally of Rosenberg actually created a 'House of Atlantis' to literally build his fantasies into the landscape. Ludwig Roselius created this site in the Böttcherstrasse in Bremen and announced:

> *The House of Atlantis is intended to make every German ask himself the question: what do you know about the proud past of your ancestors? Have you thought back to the time of Rome, Greece and Egypt; do you know that these three great cultures were originated by the men of the north, your ancestors?*

Another Atlantologist to find favour with Himmler was Edmund Kiss. Wirth had placed Atlantis between Iceland and the Azores. Kiss appeared to place it over a far wider range of geographical areas – East Africa, South America and the North Pole.

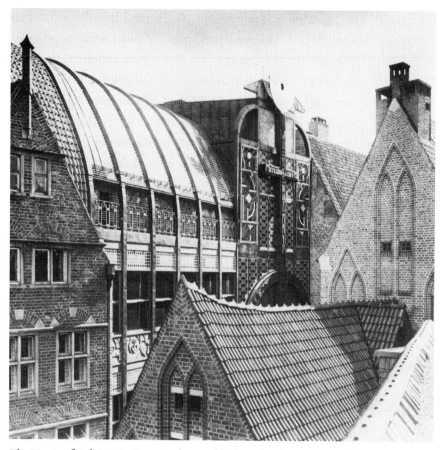

The House of Atlantis in Bremen designed by Bernhardt Hoetger in the art deco style, c.1935: largely destroyed in the war, it sported a solar disc recalling the Norse god Odin.

Kiss and his friend Arthur Posnansky examined the ruins of Tiahuanaco in Bolivia and claimed that the site had been constructed by Aryan survivors of the Atlantis cataclysm. He believed that he had discovered a stone calendar which dated back millions of years. Another 'find' on the site was a sculpture of a man's head with Aryan features. Kiss announced that the Tiahuanaco relics were 'the creation of Nordic man who arrived in the Andean highlands as representatives of a special civilization'.

There was disagreement between Wirth and Kiss over how Atlantis had met its fate. Wirth believed that a polar shift was responsible while Kiss claimed that the collapse of a previous moon upon earth had destroyed Atlantis. In 1936 Kiss was sent to Ethiopia by Himmler to find evidence for his theory but nothing was discovered during his expedition.

Perhaps the most extreme of all German Atlantologists was Karl-Georg Zschaetzsch. He claimed that the people of Atlantis were blond Aryans and that 'fiery rain' had destroyed their land. Only Wotan, his daughter and his sister remained of the true Atlantean stock.

However some non-Aryan humans had also survived and because the Aryans intermarried with these lesser breeds they became 'racially impure'. Even worse was the fact that the wicked non-Nordics also taught the virtuous Aryans to eat meat and drink beer. As if all this cloudy fantasy was not ridiculous enough Zschaetzsch concluded his book by claiming to be a direct descendant of Zeus and declared that his surname was simply the German form of the Greek god's name!

FRANCO FAVOURS THE CANARY ISLANDS

The Canary Islands were another suggested location for Atlantis or at least remnants of the continent. This theory was favoured by General Franco and following his victory in the Spanish Civil War, he approached the *Ahnenerbe* to conduct the research. The outbreak of the Second World War made it impossible for German 'experts' to participate but a Spanish archaeologist named Julio Santa Olalla was appointed to carry out investigations. Santa Olalla was a friend of Franco's and his project was approved. The Spanish excavations were funded by Himmler and many aerial photographs were taken of sites that interested the researchers. Santa Olalla liaised closely with Otto Huth who was the relevant *Ahnenerbe* official. They published the results of Santa Olalla's research and allowed him to visit Germany and give talks on his findings. Nothing of any consequence was discovered during the course of these explorations.

One of the reasons why both Franco and Himmler were so interested in the Canary Islands was the presence of physical differences between the Guanche tribes of the Canaries and the people of mainland Spain. Unlike the Spanish the Guanches have prominent cheekbones and foreheads that are pronounced and smooth-shaped. The similarities between the Guanches and the prehistoric Cro-Magnon people who entered Europe and dominated it for centuries led to the suggestion that they had made their way from Atlantis to the European continent.

When the Spanish discovered the Canaries in the fifteenth century AD they found three distinct ethnic groups on the islands. One type was olive-skinned, another had lighter skin and hair and the people in the western part of the islands were described as being fair-skinned and 'very strong, with fair hair and blue eyes'.

The Greek historian Plutarch actually referred to the inhabitants of the Canaries as Atlanteans. Other striking features of the Guanches are their use of a 'whistling language' that has been compared to bird calls and which they used to communicate with one another over great distances; their mummification of human bodies; the similarities between their writing and Egyptian hieroglyphs; the strange underground structures they built on Gran Canaria and the presence on the islands of ruins excavated from volcanic rock resembling those of Zimbabwe, Sardinia and Jericho.

The Guanches of the Canaries, the ancient Egyptians and the Araucanian Indians who lived in Tiahuanaco were also strikingly similar physically. The sandals on the feet of a statue of Chacmol at Chichen Itza are 'exact representations of those found on the feet of the Guanches, the early inhabitants of the Canary Islands'. On Hierro and Las Palmas in the Canaries stones have been discovered 'bearing sculptured symbols similar to those found on the shores of Lake Superior'.

Athanasius Kircher suggested in 1678 that the Canaries and the Azores were the last remaining parts of Atlantis. Adolf Schulten agreed that they were part of Atlantis but in his view they were only outlying areas rather than a part of the main continent.

The Guanches are an abiding source of mystery. Where did they come from? How did they get to the Canary Islands? Inevitably, some connected them with Atlantis.

THE BASQUES AND ATLANTIS

The Nazis also considered the Basques to be possible survivors of Atlantis. Their language has an affinity with some Central American tongues. Like the Aztecs the Basques worshipped a serpent and the Basque game of jai alai (also known as pelota) is similar to the Mayan game pok-a-tok.

These and other similarities led to the suggestion that the Basques were at least related to the Cro-Magnons and that both were probably remnants of the lost Atlantean civilization. Some of their customs and religious beliefs were also found among the Egyptians and the Indians of Central and South America. They are certainly completely different from any other ethnic group within Europe and their language is totally unrelated to any other European tongue.

Linguists have however discovered marked similarities between the Basque language and Central and South American languages, the tongues of the Berbers and Tuaregs of North Africa and even some words in the ancient Gaulish of France. This of course has a number of possible explanations, as languages can migrate without any corresponding racial migration, but the facts are interesting all the same. As F.W. Farrar wrote:

> What is certain about it [the Basque language] is, that its structure is polysyllabic, like the languages of America. Like them, it forms its compounds by the elimination of certain radicals in the simple words, so that ilhun, the twilight, is contracted from hill, dead, and egun, day; and belhaur, the knee, from belhar, front, and oin, leg. The fact is indisputable, and is eminently noteworthy, that while the affinities of the Basque roots have never been conclusively elucidated, there has never been any doubt that this isolated language, preserving its identity in a western corner of Europe, between two mighty kingdoms, resembles, in its grammatical structure, the aboriginal languages of the vast opposite continent (America) and those alone.

At one time the Basques were a widespread and powerful people. They colonized Italy, France, the British Isles and Scandinavia. The Greek historian Strabo described them as 'the most cultivated of all the Iberians [Spanish]; they employ the art of writing, and have written books containing memorials of ancient times, and all poems and laws set in verse, in which they claim an antiquity of six thousand years'. It has also been pointed out how many of the chants reported by the Inquisition as being used by witches were in the Basque language, which is unquestionably the oldest of all European tongues.

ANTARCTICA, ATLANTIS AND THE NAZIS

Other Nazi Atlantologists became interested in the possibilities of Antarctica. In 1938, Captain Alfred Ritscher led an expedition to the continent on the MS *Schwabenland* (Swabia). The ship was capable of carrying and launching aircraft from its decks. There were thirty-five members of the expedition, in addition to the twenty-four-man ship's crew. They left Hamburg on 17 December 1938 and arrived at Princess Martha Coast in Antarctica on 19 January 1939.

The expedition members began charting and surveying the region and planting Nazi flags on the ice along the coast. They named the area Neu Schwabenland and set up base camp before walking along the coast and staking 'claims' on various parts of the Antarctic landscape. The crews of the two seaplanes that had travelled with the ship also made a number of aerial surveys and took numerous photographs. As well as charting the area the aircraft also dropped a dozen aluminium arrows with swastikas to claim the land for Nazi Germany.

Ritscher's expedition found many ice-free parts of Antarctica and a number of lakes where the ice was thin. Vegetation was also found and aerial photography revealed signs of what appeared to be, the team excitedly declared, 'roads' beneath the ice. Caves of ice were also discovered.

These are facts upon which there is general agreement, but some people go on to make more radical claims. In the ice-caves it is alleged that evidence of an advanced ancient civilization was discovered. The Nazis are also said to have constructed an underground base in Antarctica.

Even more extravagant assertions are made concerning the fate of a German submarine. According to official records U-2015 disappeared in April 1945 somewhere in the area of Denmark. Others suggest that she smuggled the German treasury out of the country and into Argentina. It is alleged that gold and silver, looted art works, the 'blood flag' of the Nazi Party and even the Spear of Destiny all found their way into the submarine and eventually to South America. For reasons that are not made clear leading Nazis are also said to have travelled on to Antarctica and to have set up their new headquarters at the underground base allegedly constructed by Ritscher's expedition.

Conspiracy theorists have also claimed that Hitler, Bormann and various other Nazi leaders escaped to the South Pole after the fall of Germany. Some believe they went on to develop 'miracle weapons' and even flying saucers from their Antarctic base.

The research vessel MS Schwabenland *charted Antarctica, its seaplanes dropping a dozen aluminium arrows with swastikas to claim the territory for Nazi Germany.*

All of these wild claims rest upon a lack of evidence. The members of Ritscher's expedition did survey the continent by land and air but no support for the idea that they discovered any kind of previous advanced civilization there has ever been produced. Nor is it probable that any kind of Nazi 'base' in Antarctica would have been left unmolested after the defeat of Germany in 1945.

TIBET AND ATLANTIS

Tibet was also associated with Atlantis by some German 'researchers'. There had been a number of German expeditions to Tibet under Nazi leadership since 1926. The best known and most 'successful' of these took place between 1938 and 1939.

Much of the Nazi interest in Tibet stemmed from Haushofer's theories on the Aryan race's origins in what he called 'the heartland'. This area included the Gobi Desert, Tibet and the Hindu Kush. Another source was Friedrich Hielscher who was a friend of Wirth's and also worked for the *Ahnenerbe* researching runes, the symbolism of the swastika and the origins of the Aryans. Hielscher believed that Tibet held the key to the 'lost knowledge' of the Nordic race. Wirth was also convinced that Tibet had some kind of connection with Atlantis and the other related 'Aryan' factors were enough to convince Himmler to sponsor a research expedition to the country on behalf of the *Ahnenerbe*.

Ernst Schäfer was the leader in this venture. He had taken part in previous expeditions to Tibet and was well respected. His team included the 'racial researcher' Bruno Beger who believed that a 'Northern race' existed in Tibet and central Asia. Beger measured the skulls of Tibetan and Sikkimese people and declared that they were a 'hybrid' race with both European and Mongoloid features. Schäfer later wrote an account of his expedition which gave a cautious description of what had taken place. Many questions about his trip remain unanswered and certainly no trace of Atlantis seems to have been discovered in Tibet.

IMPORTANCE OF ATLANTIS TO THE NAZIS

How and why did the myth of Atlantis become so important to the Nazis? Throughout the nineteenth century it had been wildly popular in Germany and the early twentieth century saw many German researchers becoming involved in expeditions to discover its remains.

Although both Himmler's *Ahnenerbe* and Rosenberg's Amt devoted time, effort and money to their research into fantasies, they could also point to some more serious constructive work. Before the Nazis came to power there was almost no interest in German prehistory and certainly no significant public funding for archaeological research in that field. Both organizations did generate a new interest in the German past and both sponsored archaeological digs. If Himmler and Rosenberg had been conventional politicians that would have been enough to satisfy them. Sadly they were both dreamers in pursuit of a vision that could never be realized. When the results of their excavations produced nothing remotely comparable with the splendour of Greece, Rome, Egypt, Mesopotamia, India or China they simply clung to the delusion that a German Atlantis had taken the fruits of civilization to all these other people and nations.

'Racial researcher' Bruno Beger takes 'anthropological measurements' during a visit to Tibet – he declared the Tibetans and the Sikkimese people to be 'hybrid races'.

Rejecting the generally accepted view that humanity had evolved slowly towards a higher level of civilization, the *völkisch* Atlantologists declared indignantly that the reverse was true. In the dim distant past of prehistory the Aryans had founded the greatest and most advanced civilization ever seen upon earth. With the coming of the Ice Age or some kind of cosmic catastrophe this Aryan Atlantis was destroyed and only remnants of its survivors were able to preserve their knowledge and learning. Even twentieth century humans were a pale shadow of their ancestors and were only slowly beginning to approach the exalted level of their former greatness.

Even Hitler made occasional remarks suggesting that he too had swallowed these racist fantasies. Perhaps the most absurd of his comments along these lines was his statement that 'a thousand years before Rome was built, the Germanic tribes had already reached a high cultural level'. That pronouncement clearly points to a date around 1750BC, when Minoan Crete, Mycenaean Greece and Asiatic Troy all flourished with an infinitely higher 'cultural level' than anything the Germans of that period could offer in the way of competition. No doubt the comforting delusion that all of these places had received their own civilization from German survivors of Atlantis allowed him to believe such obvious nonsense.

Perhaps the final word on the Nazi obsession with Atlantis should be left to Rauschning. He said:

> At bottom every German has one foot in Atlantis, where he seeks a better fatherland and a better patrimony. This double nature of the Germans, this faculty they have of splitting their personality, which enables them to live in the real world and at the same time to project themselves into an imaginary world, is specially noticeable in Hitler and provides the key to his magic socialism.

So potent was the Atlantis myth for the Nazis that even the German Navy became caught up in it and built an auxiliary cruiser called *Atlantis* in 1937. During the Second World War it travelled over a hundred thousand miles and sank or captured twenty-two Allied ships before being finally sunk on 21 November 1941.

The 'Aryan Atlantis' in which Hitler, Himmler, Rosenberg and many other Nazi leaders believed may have been a fantasy but it 'validated' their racial prejudices and made their worst excesses praiseworthy in their eyes. To men pursuing the vision of a resurrected Atlantis the myth of the lost Nordic paradise was well worth killing and dying for.

Chapter Eight
THE REAL RAIDERS OF THE LOST ARK

ONE OF THE GREATEST ironies in history is that a movement which hated Christianity and Judaism became obsessed with the sacred relics of both religions. As a young man in Vienna, Hitler became fascinated by the Lance of St Maurice in the Hofburg Museum. This artefact is better known as 'the Holy Lance' or 'the Spear of Destiny' and is alleged to have been the weapon with which the Roman centurion Longinus pierced the side of Jesus as he hung on the Cross at Calvary.

THE SPEAR OF DESTINY

A number of different weapons are claimed to be the 'true' spear. One is held in the Vatican and was first described in AD570 by a pilgrim to Jerusalem who saw it in the Basilica of Mount Zion. Other visitors of the same period also mention its presence in Jerusalem. How authentic a relic it was is open to question as even at this comparatively early stage in Church history, the faking of sacred objects to attract donations was already a growing problem. During the wars between the Byzantine and Persian empires, Persian troops captured Jerusalem and took its treasures back to Iran. The point of the lance was broken off and carried back to Constantinople. In the twelfth century this point was sold to King Louis IX of France who placed it in the Sainte Chapelle in Paris. It disappeared during the French Revolution and has never been seen again.

The shaft of the lance is alleged to have fared rather better. A pilgrim claimed to have seen it in AD670 at the Church of the Holy Sepulchre in Jerusalem. Visitors to Constantinople in the eighth century also claimed to have seen the lance in a variety of different churches. After the city was captured by the Turks it was sent by Sultan Beyezid II to the Pope and has remained in the Vatican ever since. The Catholic Church makes no claims either way about the authenticity of its status as a holy relic.

A lance held in Armenia is also claimed to be the spear that pierced the side of Jesus and is on display in a museum within the country. It is alleged that the apostle Thaddeus took it to the country although there is no record of its existence before the thirteenth century.

THE HOLY LANCE IN THE HOFBURG MUSEUM

The main contender for authentic status is the Holy Lance held by the Hofburg Museum in Vienna. It is this lance that has become known as the 'Spear of Destiny' and is associated with Hitler. The first unambiguous mention of this relic is in the early tenth century AD when it was in the possession of the Holy Roman Emperor Otto I. At various times it was

Rommel and his Afrika Korps came close to fitting the image of Raiders of the Lost Ark, *but the real Nazis were looking for archaeological artefacts far closer to home.*

housed in Prague and Nuremberg but from 1796 it was kept in Vienna. It remained there until the *Anschluss* with Germany in 1938, when it was housed in Nuremberg before being hidden as Allied troops invaded the country. Some American soldiers discovered its hiding place and it was returned to Austria after the end of the Second World War.

It is highly probable that the lance in Vienna is the oldest of the three claimants, although neither of its rivals has been examined by experts. The Hofburg spear has been scientifically tested by the metallurgist Dr Robert Feather and he dated it to the seventh century AD. That is of course far too late for it to have been the lance that pierced the side of Jesus. However an intriguing anomaly was found during the course of testing. It was discovered that an iron pin within the blade could be from the first century AD. The tradition has always been that the Hofburg Lance incorporated a nail from the Crucifixion.

If that claim is true then how did a first century nail survive and come to be hammered into a seventh century spear? The answer appears to lie with the rulers of Italy at that time. In the seventh century the country was ruled by the Lombard kings whose coronation ceremony involved grasping a ceremonial lance. The Lombard capital was Milan and the Roman Emperor Constantine's mother is known to have brought to the city what was alleged to be a nail from the Crucifixion. The kings might have wanted to give their royal line additional sanctity by incorporating within the lance a nail from the Cross. When Charlemagne conquered the Lombards in the eighth century he took possession of the lance which eventually became part of the Holy Roman Empire's regalia and so passed into the possession of the Austrian royal house.

Whatever the true facts there is no doubt that the Holy Lance exercised a powerful fascination upon many people. One of them was Hitler's favourite composer Richard Wagner. In *Parsifal* Wagner equates the lance with the spear that wounds the Fisher King and is lost by the knights of the Grail before being recovered by Parsifal.

HITLER AND THE HOLY LANCE

There is no question but that Hitler saw the spear in the Hofburg Museum during his time in Vienna, but the extent to which his discovery of it influenced his attitudes and behaviour has been fiercely disputed. According to Trevor Ravenscroft the spear had a profound effect upon him and represented the beginning of his path into occultism and darkness. There is no doubt that Hitler was aware of the religious associations of the object and it is highly probable that once he became German Chancellor his thoughts turned towards acquiring it for Germany. Many conquerors throughout history have sought to gain possession of sacred objects from rival religions and Hitler's undoubted desire to own the spear would have been in the same tradition of neutralizing the 'power' of such an object.

On the other hand there are serious problems with accepting Ravenscroft's account of Hitler's involvement with the spear during his youth in Vienna. To begin with his assertions about Hitler rest solely upon the testimony of Dr Walter Stein, so he is reporting an account remembered many years after the event. In such circumstances all kinds of mistakes and exaggerations can creep into a story. What Ravenscroft gives us is an account of what he says Stein told him about what Hitler said and did many years before.

An additional problem is that parts of Ravenscroft's story have been shown to be questionable. There is no record in Vienna of a bookshop belonging to an Ernst Pretzsche. The description Ravenscroft gives of Pretzsche's shop is also sufficiently similar to one in Lytton's occult novel *Zanoni* to raise further doubts.

It has also been suggested that Stein and Hitler would never have formed the close relationship that Ravenscroft described them as having. Stein was Jewish and Hitler was of course a fanatical anti-Semite. That particular objection holds little validity.

To begin with Stein was a man deeply immersed in *völkisch* and occult fantasies. He wrote extensively on Atlantis, mythology and the idea of an ancient civilization at the North Pole. Stein also appeared to share the idea of 'racial souls', so the mental universe in which he operated was certainly one which Hitler could easily have shared.

More importantly there is no evidence of any anti-Semitic attitudes or remarks by Hitler earlier than 1919. Those who knew him before that period agree that his favourite actors and comedians were Jewish and that although he loved Wagner's music best of all he also enjoyed listening to Mendelssohn, Lehár and Mahler. One of his few friends during this time was Jewish and the first girl he fell in love with was Jewish. He was also an active and enthusiastic supporter of Kurt Eisner, the Jewish leader of 'Soviet Bavaria'. Hitler was a member of a Soldiers' Council in Munich and attended Eisner's funeral. Even during his days as German leader he never condemned Eisner and one of his first acts as Chancellor was to arrest the man who assassinated him. The idea that Hitler was anti-Semitic before 1919 is flatly contradicted by the available evidence.

None of these things mean that Ravenscroft's accounts of the various meetings between Stein and Hitler are literal descriptions of what may have taken place and may have been said between them. However, it is entirely possible that two men as steeped in *völkisch* fantasies as Stein and Hitler did meet in Vienna and may well have discussed the 'mystical' significance of the spear. It would be dangerous to go beyond that but while it is entirely probable that much if not most of Ravenscroft's account is imaginative reconstruction it is also highly likely that it contains a core of truth. Hitler's first act on entering Vienna was to remove the spear from the Hofburg Museum and take it back to Nuremberg, so it clearly held a special significance in his eyes.

As a final note on the question of Hitler and the 'Spear of Destiny', it has been claimed that Picasso's *Guernica* contains coded messages which describe a psychic battle between Hitler and the Spanish artist, involving the lance. It is alleged that these hidden 'messages' describe events in Hitler's life as well as referring to aspects of Wagner's *Parsifal*. The idea of a 'Picasso code' seems highly implausible but it is certainly a new addition to the corpus of myth surrounding the 'Spear of Destiny'.

THE LOST ARK OF THE COVENANT

The lost Ark of the Covenant was once the most sacred relic in Judaism. According to the *Book of Exodus* it was a chest containing the stone tablets on which the Ten Commandments were written and it dated back to the time of the Israelites' captivity in Egypt. Exodus claims that Moses was directed to construct it when God spoke to him on Mount Sinai and that during the journey out of Egypt the priests carried the Ark in front of the Israelites as they passed. Once the Ark had been built God was able to communicate directly with Moses 'from between the two cherubim' that decorated the chest.

The Ark was made of shittim wood and plated with gold. A crown of gold was also placed all around it with four golden rings attached, two on either side. The wooden staves – themselves plated with gold – were then inserted for the purpose of carrying the Ark. Golden cherubim were set in a cover of gold that was placed on top of the Ark. Finally the chest was covered with a veil.

During its time in Israel it was moved to a number of locations. At one point it was captured by the Philistines but returned after seven months. When Solomon built his Temple, it contained an inner room called 'the Holy of Holies' within which the Ark was placed.

When the Babylonians conquered Judah in 586BC they destroyed the city of Jerusalem and the Temple. From that point onwards the Ark vanishes from the pages of history. Both the Jewish apocryphal books and the rabbinical traditions disagree over its final destiny. The First Book of Esdras says that the Babylonians:

> took all the holy vessels of the Lord, both great and small, and the Ark of God, and the king's treasures, and carried them away to Babylon.

Some rabbis agree with this interpretation while others declare that the Ark was hidden to prevent its capture. The apocryphal book the Second Book of Maccabees also takes that view, declaring that Jeremiah removed the Ark, the tent and the altar of incense to 'the mountain of God' where he sealed the treasures within a cave. Jeremiah then announced:

> the place shall remain unknown until God gathers His people together again and shows His mercy, and then the Lord will disclose these things, and the glory of the Lord and the cloud shall appear, as they were shown in the case of Moses, and as Solomon asked that the place be specially consecrated.

The general belief is that the Ark contained only the tablets of stone upon which the Ten Commandments were written but even the Bible is not consistent in its description of the contents. Exodus and Kings agree with that description but Numbers claims that it also held Aaron's rod, the first Torah scroll and a jar of manna. In the New Testament the Epistle to the Hebrews says that it contained 'the golden pot that had manna, and Aaron's rod that budded, and the tablets of the Covenant'.

In the Book of Revelation it is stated that both the Temple and the Ark are in heaven.

There is no doubt that the Ark disappeared during the Babylonian capture of Jerusalem. A bewildering variety of locations have been suggested as its 'true' resting place. The earliest proposed site for the Ark is given in the *Second Book of Maccabees*. That placed it within a cave on Mount Nebo in Jordan but no evidence of its presence there has ever been found.

The Coptic Church in Ethiopia claims that it rests within a treasury near the Church of Our Lady Mary of Zion in Axum. This assertion dates back to the twelfth century AD and its best known expression is in the *Kebra Nagast* which was written around a hundred years later. The Ethiopians claim that their monarchy was descended from Solomon and the Queen of Sheba and that the ark in their possession is the 'true' Ark of the Covenant. The ark which remained behind in Solomon's

The Siege of Jericho: the Ark of the Covenant was always wrapped in a veil when transported and its light concealed from the eyes of the priests who carried it.

Temple was only a copy. Periodically patriarchs of the Coptic Church announce that they will 'unveil' the Ark of the Covenant but so far none of these promises have been fulfilled. The true date of the Ethiopian ark remains unknown.

Another favoured location is Zimbabwe where the Lemba people claim that their ancestors brought it to the country and hid it within a cave in the Dumghe Mountains. According to Lemba traditions the Ark was ferried overseas from Yemen at around the time the Zimbabwean civilization was coming to its close. The tribe members say that soon after its arrival in the country it 'self-destructed'. They built a replacement ark using a core from the original object. The replica ark is now in the Museum of Human Sciences in Harare and has been carbon dated to AD1350. This date corresponds with the fall of the Zimbabwean civilization.

Some Catholics claim that the Ark is housed in the Basilica of St John Lateran in Rome. Other authors believe that the Knights Templar discovered it in the Holy Land after which it was moved. Locations suggested for its new 'home' include Chartres Cathedral, Rennes-le-Château, Warwickshire in England and even America. Some British Israelites suggest that it was taken to Ireland by Jeremiah and is buried under a hill at Tara.

All of these locations are highly speculative and the two most probable ones are that either the Ark was looted by the Babylonians and subsequently destroyed or that it was hidden in the region of Mount Nebo. It is certainly hard to see how it could have travelled all the way to Yemen or Ethiopia given the urgent military situation at the time of its disappearance.

In the film *Raiders of the Lost Ark* the hero attempts to prevent the Nazis gaining possession of the Ark of the Covenant. Even though this is a Hollywood adventure film the story was not spun out of whole cloth. The Nazis really did spend time and money on trying to track down sacred relics and legendary objects such as the Ark and the Holy Grail.

There was a certain amount of overlapping in both these 'quests' which were mainly funded by the *Ahnenerbe* and at least one of which involved the same individual. Otto Rahn was primarily associated with the quest for the Grail but it is alleged that he also became involved in searching for the Ark of the Covenant. The possible connection of both with the medieval heretics known as the Cathars was the basis on which a kind of mission of discovery with two possible 'targets' was undertaken. Both Himmler and Rosenberg shared an obsession with the Cathars, so funding for any research with alleged connections to them would always be forthcoming.

THE NAZIS TRY TO FIND THE ARK

When Mussolini conquered Ethiopia in 1936 he was asked to discover the truth about the Ark. The *Ahnenerbe*'s Edmund Kiss visited the country and added the search for the Ark to his other occult preoccupations. It is clear that the object which the Coptic Church claims to be the Ark did not find favour with the Nazi researchers and they turned their attention to other possible sites.

They do not seem to have considered Ireland a likely location but they certainly investigated France and Spain. Iraq was also regarded as a possibility but surprisingly no attention appears to have been given to the Zimbabwean ark.

All of the theories placing the Ark in Europe rest on the belief that either the Cathars or the Knights Templar were involved in its removal or concealment. It is just possible to imagine the Templars having a connection with such an enterprise as they had lived, fought and excavated in the Holy Land. They also possessed a sizeable fleet so they could conceivably have carried away the Ark to their main power base in France. Although it is a remote possibility, it is highly unlikely that they did so. The suggestion that they might have been responsible is comparatively recent and neither their defenders nor their detractors ever alleged any connection between the Templars and the Ark.

It is even less plausible to associate the Cathars with the Ark of the Covenant. They were a viciously anti-Semitic sect who believed that the Jews were literally children of the Devil and that they worshipped Satan. In addition the majority of Cathars were poor and would not have possessed the resources to discover, transfer and conceal such an important object.

Rahn appears to have failed to either locate the Ark during the course of his researches or establish any connection between it and the Cathars. He believed he had been more successful in terms of the Holy Grail.

Before turning to the Nazi Grail quest it is necessary to consider briefly the claims made by Howard Buechner that the SS Colonel Otto Skorzeny recovered the Ark and the Grail from the south of France in 1944. There is no evidence for this claim and Skorzeny never mentioned this particular 'exploit' either in his books or privately. Although it is an entertaining theory, it is almost certainly mistaken.

OTTO RAHN AND THE QUEST FOR THE HOLY GRAIL

Most of the Nazi Grail quest involves Otto Rahn in some respect. As a child, his favourite reading was German, Scandinavian, Greek and Roman mythology. Rahn's niece also claimed that he possessed 'second sight'. Before long he became obsessed with the *Nibelungenlied* and the stories of Lohengrin and Parsifal. At university he developed a new interest in the Cathars which he described as 'a subject that completely captivated me'.

Rahn believed that the thirteenth-century German poem *Parzival* was connected with the Cathars' beliefs. He concluded that the sect had been in possession of a sacred relic and that the Grail Castle of Munsálvaesche described in the poem was based upon the Cathar stronghold of Montségur. Rahn regarded the Cathars as the last custodians of the Grail and became obsessed with the sect. He planned to write a dissertation on Guyot of Provence, a Troubadour who is generally regarded as the origin of the author Kyot, on whose lost poem about the Grail Wolfram von Eschenbach based his *Parzival*. Wagner's opera brought Wolfram's poem firmly into the public eye and Rahn became convinced that the earlier work held vital clues to the Grail quest on which he had embarked and which dominated the rest of his life.

Rahn became so deeply immersed in his researches into the Cathars that he ended up sharing their religious views. In spite of the fact that all the evidence points to an entirely different conclusion, he was convinced that the Cathar beliefs were derived from Druidism. It is

Otto Rahn became obsessed with the Nibelungenlied, *the epic poem in which dragon-slayer Siegfried (above) meets Kriemhild, who dreamt of a falcon killed by two eagles.*

certainly true that the Grail legend has elements of Druidic thought within it because of its Celtic origins, but there is little similarity between the life-affirming teachings of Druidism and the world-denial of the Cathars.

His subsidiary claim that the Troubadours and the Minnesingers were heavily influenced by Catharism or were even active members of the sect is rather more plausible. There is no doubt that the Troubadours were exposed to a range of unorthodox ideas via northern Spain and to a lesser extent the Crusades, Italy and even Eastern Europe. One of the reasons why the Catholic Church devoted seven centuries to the persecution of heretics was precisely because it felt its grip on power loosening. The Troubadours were particularly influenced by unorthodox ideas from Spanish and Italian sources and many of those ultimately derived from the Middle East via the Western Muslim Empire in Spain.

The Troubadours were famous for their courtly love poetry, but there is considerable truth in the view held by Rahn and the Italian fascist fellow-traveller Julius Evola that much of their love poetry was coded religious verse with Sophia, the alleged female principle of Divine Wisdom, being the true 'beloved' of the poets. Certainly the Persian mystic Omar Khayyam used wine and love in a similar way to symbolize his Sufi religious beliefs.

Rahn agreed with the Cathars that the world is a continual struggle between good and evil. As they saw the world as evil it could not have been created by God but must have been the work of the Devil. The belief that God had created the world made Christians Devil-worshippers in the eyes of the Cathars. The Cathars denounced Christians for not understanding that it was not only possible but desirable to try to escape from life and return to the primeval union with God which had existed before Creation.

RAHN LOOKS FOR THE GRAIL IN FRANCE

Rahn's identification with the Cathars was already almost total when he visited France in 1929. He settled in the village of Lavelanet and began a systematic exploration of Montségur and the caves in the vicinity. Rahn also visited the city of Carcassonne and the church of Rennes-le-Château.

He believed that there was a sacred geometry within Montségur that was connected with the rising of the sun and its relationship to nearby sacred sites. He also discovered a number of secret underground tunnels and became convinced that somewhere within them the Cathar treasure was located.

He learned to speak the Provençal dialect of French and talked with many local people.

One of his most important contacts was Maurice Magre. He was the author of a number of works on the sect of which the best – perhaps because it is not solely concerned with them – is *Return of the Magi*.

There is no doubt however that his *Treasure of the Albigensians* fired Rahn's heavy imagination more than any other book.

Rahn became convinced that Wolfram's Munsalvaesche (Wagner's Monsalvat) was simply a coded name for the Cathar castle of Montségur. He also believed that Wolfram's poem expressed Cathar ideas, although most scholars disagreed with him. From another Cathar enthusiast, Antonin Gabal, Rahn adopted the idea that the sect had retreated into subterranean churches.

Rahn explored the caves of Sabarthes to the south of Montségur and paid particular attention to the Lombrives cavern, which the locals nicknamed 'the cathedral'. He was deeply impressed by the cave and gave the following description of it:

In time out of mind, in an epoch whose remoteness has been barely touched by modern historical science, it was used as a temple consecrated to the Iberian God Illhomber, God of the Sun. Between two monoliths one of which had crumbled, the steep path leads into the giant vestibule of the cathedral of Lombrives. Between the stalagmites of white limestone, between walls of a deep brown colour and the brilliant rock crystal, the path leads down into the bowels of the mountain. A hall 200 feet in height served as a cathedral for the heretics. Deeply stirred, I walked through the crystal halls and marble crypts. My hands put aside the bones of fallen pure ones and knights.

Rahn claimed that Esclarmonde d'Alion was the 'keeper of the Grail' and when Montségur was about to fall she 'threw the sacred jewel [the Grail] into the depths of the mountain. The mountain closed up again and in this manner was the Grail saved'. He confused Esclarmonde d'Alion with her aunt Esclarmonde de Foix, who built Montségur but was already dead when the fortress fell.

Within the caves of Sabarthes Rahn found many hidden chambers where the walls were covered in Templar and Cathar symbols. He was convinced of the relationship between the two movements, although most historians disagreed. On the stone wall of one part of a cave was the drawing of a lance. Rahn immediately leapt to the conclusion that the image represented the wounded 'Fisher King' of Grail legend, but a more probable explanation is that it was a symbol of the Templar knights for whom a lance was simply a weapon.

Völkisch occultists were convinced that the Grail was associated with the Templars and that King Arthur represented the Arctic Circle. They used this as a further argument in favour of their belief in a northern Atlantis.

MONTSÉGUR CASTLE

Much of Rahn's quest centred on Montségur. The castle stood on the highest point in the vicinity, above the valleys which themselves were honeycombed with rocks and above the pine forests and mountain waterfalls.

During the long wars in the south of France where the Catholic Church gradually destroyed the power of Catharism the fortress of Montségur held out to the bitter end. It contained not only the leading nobles and clergy of the religion but also its treasure.

In the end Montségur was the only remaining Cathar stronghold. An army besieged it for two years before all but a handful surrendered.

A knight's cross carved into a rock at Montségur.

The remnants escaped down a narrow pathway and took refuge in a cave to which some say they also moved the Cathar treasure. In some stories this is alleged to have been buried in the cave of Ornolhac on the edge of the forest of Sarrelongue in the region of Sabartez.

The entrance to the cave was halfway up the mountainside and their secret hiding place was so far beneath the ground that the troops of the Inquisition were unable to enter. Using ladders the Cathars withdrew to an even deeper and more remote cave. Unable to either capture the Cathars or recover their treasure the troops sealed off the entrance to the cave. The inhabitants died inside the deep cavern and with them perished the secret of their treasure.

THE LOST TREASURE OF THE CATHARS

Over the centuries that followed this tragic event many people searched in vain for the hidden cave and its lost treasure. Rahn had a passionate desire to uncover the final resting place of the last adherents of Catharism and if possible recover their hidden secrets.

What was the mysterious treasure of the Cathars? Was it gold, jewellery or similarly valuable items? Was it a holy book or books? Was it a sacred object of some description or was it something non-material, a hidden knowledge that had somehow survived the persecution?

In the 1930s there were many Cathar enthusiasts in France and each one seemed to have a different theory about the true nature of the treasure. Some believed that it was a bowl, a plate, a cup, a book, a jewel or a stone. Wolfram claimed that the owner of the Grail 'would have eternal life and would be healed'.

Rahn met with a woman known as Miriam de Pujol-Murat, a countess who owned the Château of Lordat and claimed to be a direct descendant of Esclarmonde de Foix, the founder of Montségur. Various archaeological excavations took place within her grounds with the objects of the dig ranging from the tomb of the founder of the Rosicrucian Order to the alleged 'lost' Gospel of St John. Rahn's principal activities took place in the caves and it was in the grotto of Fontanet that he discovered some meteorites which were allegedly sacred to the ancient Mother Goddess Cybele. He identified them with the 'lapis exillis' spoken of in Wolfram's poem and described as a 'hard, dark stone'. Rahn's fellow-enthusiast Gadal called them the 'Pyrenean Grail'.

In 1932, an enigmatic letter from the French author Isabelle Sandy declared that 'a valuable treasure has been returned to us, without diplomats and without fuss and that is the result of an incomparable success'. As Rahn was staying with Sandy at the time, many people believe that Rahn had found the Grail and given it to Gadal's neo-Cathar secret society. This seems unlikely as Rahn's quest for the Grail continued, and in 1933 he visited Germelshausen in Germany, the alleged birthplace of the founder of the Rosicrucian Order. Then he went to Spain where he visited the monastery of Montserrat, which is also a candidate for the location of the Grail castle. As Sandy gave no hint of what it was that had been recovered and as Rahn himself implied in his first book that the Grail was a meteorite the story seems highly improbable.

He spent the next few years in France researching the Cathars before returning to Germany in 1933. The publication in 1934 of his first book on the subject brought him to the attention of Himmler. He was recruited into the SS and promptly despatched to carry out *Ahnenerbe* research in France, Italy and Iceland. As a result of his travels he published a second book in 1936 summarizing the results of his work.

Some believe that Otto Rahn found the Grail and took it back to Germany. Others think he found it but kept his discovery secret. Most likely of all is that he found nothing at all in spite of his years of searching. Whatever the truth is, he was found frozen to death on a mountain in 1939 and had almost certainly committed suicide.

MONTSERRAT ABBEY

In 1940 Himmler visited an abbey in Spain which has also been suggested as a possible custodian of the Holy Grail. Like Montségur in France, the abbey of Montserrat has been identified by some with the

Munsalvaesche Castle of *Parzival*. Montserrat is certainly a fascinating place, with the abbey nestling among the rocks of the high Montserrat mountain and noted for its Black Madonna. Spain at that time had many Troubadours and also many sympathizers with the Cathar faith. Beyond that it is impossible to establish any kind of connection with either the Grail or the lost Cathar treasure. Himmler came to the abbey and investigated the claims but left empty-handed.

At some unspecified point during the Second World War local tradition speaks of a Nazi U-boat that sailed up the River Clyde near Greenock in Scotland in search of the Holy Grail. Many suggest that Rahn was on board but as he had died in 1939, his involvement would have been impossible. There are certainly local associations with both the Templars and Arthurian legend, in addition to a medieval well alleged to possess healing powers, and these factors may have attracted the interest of the *Ahnenerbe*. This local legend has never been verified but it adds another layer of mystery to the Nazi quest for the Holy Grail. Considering the overwhelming association of the Grail with Britain it is surprising that the *Ahnenerbe* did not attempt to carry out research

Montserrat Abbey in its spectacularly beautiful setting high up in the mountains, but has it ever been the location of the Holy Grail?

in the country at least before the war. Instead they were mesmerized by alleged Cathar connections into investigating France, Spain, Italy and even Iceland. Of course the Grail – if it ever existed – was lost as a human object long ago and all the effort that the Nazis devoted to searching for it was utterly wasted.

Chapter Nine

'ARYAN SCIENCE' IN THE THIRD REICH

THROUGHOUT THE NINETEENTH CENTURY, German scientists and mathematicians were world leaders in research, development and discovery. They did as much as the scientists of other countries to separate out authentic fields of study from areas of 'pseudo-science'.

With the coming of Hitler to power, that changed radically. An active campaign against Jewish scientists led to the majority of them leaving the country, and the theory of relativity came under sustained attack. A whole range of pseudo-scientific ideas that had been quietly relegated to the fringes came back into fashion. It was not simply that orthodox science was badly affected by the hostility towards Jewish scientists, and even towards those areas of science such as relativity or quantum physics where Jews had contributed disproportionately to their creation and development. Ideas that had either long since been discarded as unscientific, or new ones that were dubiously scientific, became not simply fashionable within Nazi Germany, but were even regarded as being more scientific than the theories that they had replaced.

RACE SCIENCE

The most dominant of these under the Nazis was 'race science'. This particular subject was invented in the nineteenth century by Darwin's cousin Sir Francis Galton. What Galton called 'eugenics' spread rapidly and was particularly popular in Germany and America. Both the horrors of the Final Solution and the selective breeding programme of the *Lebensborn* were firmly based upon eugenic principles and to an extent were implicit within its philosophy. Galton's belief that 'racial improvement' could be conducted on the same basis as breeding plants or animals inspired a whole new group of 'racial researchers'. Geoffrey Field described it thus:

> *scores of researchers, clutching complicated callipers, craniometers, spirometers, and other sundry gauges that measured scientific ingenuity more than anatomy, scoured the countryside weighing skulls, examining bones, classifying hair and eye colour and skin pigmentation, and measuring noses, ears, heads, and every other attribute of the physical frame. From the data accumulated, large numbers of racial taxonomies were invented.*

It was soon 'clear' to these researchers that the colour of a person's skin 'determined' their 'biological superiority'.

The white races were 'clearly' the 'fittest' and non-whites were 'weaker'. In addition to this nonsensical elevation of skin colour into a criterion of superiority the 'race scientists' also declared that such qualities as courage, competitiveness and self-assertion were 'desirable', while altruism, compromise and compassion were 'biologically undesirable'. This philosophy was best expressed in a notorious saying of the time, 'the weakest go to the wall'.

Galton believed that the 'fittest' should be encouraged to have children and the 'less fit' should be actively discouraged, if necessary through a programme of compulsory sterilization. His friend Karl Pearson argued that nations were 'organic wholes' and that they could only survive if the people who lived there were 'the fittest'. Class conflict had to be ruthlessly destroyed and replaced with a socialist state where all co-operated for the greater good. Pearson's theories were nicknamed 'national socialism' and like Galton's views greatly influenced Nazi 'race scientists'.

SETTLEMENT ARCHAEOLOGY

Both pseudo-history and race science were combined in the theories of Gustaf Kossinna. He was the most famous prehistorian of his time and created a discipline he called 'settlement archaeology'. Kossinna believed that the earliest Aryans were north Germans in the region of Schleswig-Holstein.

His theory of settlement archaeology claimed that the artefacts found during the excavation of a site demonstrated the ethnic make-up of its population. Kossinna declared that 'sharply defined archaeological cultural areas correspond unquestionably with the area of particular people or tribes'. He believed not simply that all German-speaking people formed a unified national identity but that any area that had been occupied by their ancestors also belonged to Germans by right.

Kossinna not only claimed that the Aryan race was superior to all others but also that the original Aryans were German. His theories declared that the true history of the ancient world was the German gift of civilization to lesser races. In his view culture developed through 'a process whereby influences, ideas and models were passed on by more advanced peoples to the less advanced with which they came into contact' and that this superiority derived from their Nordic origins.

In Kossinna's account of history the German people stood supreme. He declared that 'Germanic people were never destroyers of culture, unlike the Romans – and the French in recent times'. Instead he claimed that the Germans had given civilization to the Greeks and the Romans mainly through their migrations across Europe.

All this fantastic rewriting of history from the viewpoint of German *völkisch* imperialism made Kossinna's ideas enormously popular with the Nazis. Unsurprisingly he was a strong supporter of Hitler, and both Rosenberg and Himmler were profoundly influenced by his mythologized racial account of a glorious German past.

MADISON GRANT AND NORDIC FANTASIES

There were many other influences on 'race science' but the reality is that ideas of this type were not only intellectually respectable in the West right across the other political divides but were also actively practised in many countries. The United States produced two 'thinkers' – Madison Grant and Margaret Sanger – who were not only direct influences on Hitler's racism but also succeeded in introducing various 'programmes' and 'experiments' using prisoners, African-Americans and women as guinea pigs to test their theories.

Grant was best known for his 1916 book *The Passing of the Great Race*. Like Kossinna, whose ideas influenced him greatly, Grant interpreted history and anthropology along racial lines. He declared that race was the primary factor in the emergence and establishment of civilization and that what he called the Nordic race had essentially brought this gift to the rest of the world.

Grant demanded the complete segregation of all racial types, the placing of inferior races into ghettos and ultimately the elimination of 'worthless race types'. He wrote:

A rigid system of selection through the elimination of those who are weak or unfit – in other words social failures – would solve the whole question in one hundred years, as well as enable us to get rid of all the undesirables who crowd our jails, hospitals and insane asylums. The individual himself can be nourished, educated and protected by the community during his lifetime, but the state through sterilization must see to it that his line stops with him, or else future generations will be cursed with an ever increasing load of misguided sentimentalism. This is a practical, merciful and inevitable solution of the whole problem, and can be applied to an ever widening circle of social discards, beginning

always with the criminal, the diseased, and the insane, and extending
gradually to types which may be called weaklings rather than defectives,
and perhaps ultimately to worthless race types.

Grant was not content to declare that the white race was the pinnacle of superiority but insisted that there were three sub-groups within it, with the Nordic people of northern Europe at the top of the tree. Below them came the Mediterraneans found in southern Europe, the Middle East and North Africa. At the very bottom of Grant's pile were the Alpines, dwellers in central Europe and western Asia. Grant believed that the original home of the Nordics had been Poland, Russia and eastern Germany and that they had spread out from these regions to colonize Scandinavia.

He described Nordics as 'a race of soldiers, sailors, adventurers and explorers but above all, rulers, organizers and aristocrats'. By contrast the Alpines had an 'essentially peasant character'. Ironically Hitler was a characteristically Alpine type, a fact often joked about by many Germans.

In spite of his unfortunate inability to live up to his own racial ideals, Hitler was obsessed with this sort of racial mythology. Grant's ideas spread like wildfire among *völkisch* German thinkers, although with the exception of Rosenberg, they tended to use the term Aryan rather than Nordic. His claim that the Nordics were on the point of committing 'race suicide' by mixing with inferior races and allowing them to outbreed the superior ones was one that Hitler echoed relentlessly in his own propaganda. Hitler was so inspired by Grant that when he became Chancellor, *The Passing of the Great Race* was the first non-German book ordered to be printed by the Nazis. He wrote to Grant and told him that 'the book is my Bible'.

MARGARET SANGER AND EUGENICS
Margaret Sanger is best remembered today as a fierce advocate of birth control. Unlike Grant, whose ideas have long ceased to be taken

seriously, Sanger has been sanitized and reinvented as a feminist icon in rather the same way that the Nazi feminist Lydia Gottschewski has been transformed into 'a German political activist'. Of course Sanger *was* a strong supporter of birth control but she also stood shoulder to shoulder with Grant and other racial scientists. She despised black people and her principal reason for advocating contraception was her belief that it would 'assist the race towards the elimination of the unfit'. Sanger believed that preventing the reproduction of unfit breeding stock would improve hereditary traits in human beings by gradually eliminating defective genes.

Her proposals for achieving this goal were stringent immigration control, extensive promotion of birth control and compulsory sterilization for the unfit. She did at least disagree with those eugenicists who wanted the unfit to be subject to compulsory euthanasia but her obsession with 'racial betterment' and her determination to exclude immigrants 'whose condition is known to be detrimental to the stamina of the race' rather spoilt the effect of her condemnation of killing. Sanger asserted that fair-skinned people were inherently superior to those with darker skin. She even wrote in a letter 'we do not want the word to go out that we want to exterminate the Negro population'. As the American Black Power leader Angela Davis pointed out, this quote, along with other evidence about Sanger's attitudes to black people, means and can only mean the genocide by stealth of an entire race.

Even in Britain such plans were followed through, though to a lesser extent and for a shorter period of time. Hitler praised Sanger and said privately that she had been one of his inspirations for the Final Solution. Although the Nazis took 'race science' to new depths of absurdity and brutality, it is only fair to say that in their ideas on race they largely reflected the dominant prejudices of their time.

GEOPOLITICS AND *LEBENSRAUM*

Geopolitics was a pseudo-science invented by the British writer Sir Halford Mackinder to provide an ideological justification for British imperialism. His ideas became popular in Germany where they were turned on their head to support a programme of German expansion. The leading German 'expert' on geopolitics was Haushofer, whose term *Lebensraum* – living-space – became a key concept in German military and foreign policy.

Perhaps surprisingly for a member of a nation whose survival had always depended on its mastery of the sea, Mackinder paid more attention to land-based warfare. His highly selective and dubious interpretation of history led him to conclude that a swathe of land stretching from the Rhine in the west to Tibet and Mongolia in the east represented the 'heartland' and whoever controlled that territory dominated the world. If they had come up against Mackinder's theories, Alexander the Great, Julius Caesar and many other rulers of vast empires might well have wondered how they had managed

Karl Haushofer with Gerhard Wagner, the Nazi doctors' leader responsible for euthanasia and sterilization for Jews and the disabled, Rudolf Hess and Prinz zu Wied, 1935.

to dominate the known world without controlling the heartland. Mackinder believed that great nations were forced by the increase in their population to seek new territory to settle their excess people and conquer new territory for their empires.

Haushofer's concept of geopolitics was even cruder and more simplistic than Mackinder's. Hess was totally convinced of both the truth of *Lebensraum* and its vital importance for the future direction of Germany. While Hitler and Hess were in prison Haushofer came to visit them and he fired Hitler with enthusiasm for a geopolitical strategy.

GERMAN FOREIGN POLICY

Ever since Germany had become a nation there had always been three schools of thought about the direction its foreign policy should take. In spite of having fought three successful wars Bismarck advocated a peaceful approach to foreign relations and, crucially, a policy of friendship with Russia, while displaying a lack of interest in expanding German territory either within Europe or overseas. The second school was represented by Bismarck's successor as Chancellor, Leo von Caprivi, and favoured German expansion overseas and acquiring colonies for the nation. The third school was represented by Theobald von Bethmann-Hollweg, Chancellor at the outbreak of the First World War, and favoured a policy of expansion eastwards and acquiring territory from Russia and the countries of Eastern Europe.

Hitler's own preference in foreign policy was for Bethmann-Hollweg's approach. He had little real interest in recovering the German colonies in Africa and Asia that had been lost after the Treaty of Versailles but was determined to wrest vast territory from Russia and to become master of the whole of Eastern Europe. This obsession meant that war with the Soviet Union would inevitably come, and even the two-year Nazi–Soviet Pact was simply a tactical manoeuvre rather than – as most German Foreign Office ministers hoped – representing a genuine shift in policy.

When Hitler became Chancellor he made available vast sums of public money to Haushofer's Institute of Geopolitics in Munich. Haushofer used his institute to research the strengths and weaknesses of other countries, in-depth psychological profiles of leading political and military figures and even climatic conditions. He employed a staff of over a thousand historians, psychologists, meteorologists, economists, physicists, geographers and military experts to evaluate the data his institute processed.

HAUSHOFER'S GEOPOLITICAL PREDICTIONS

As a result of this research Haushofer advised Hitler on the 'correct course of action' and its likely results. In 1938 army chiefs were convinced that Britain and France would go to war over Czechoslovakia; Haushofer assured Hitler that they would not fight. In 1939 the generals were convinced that their tanks would become stuck in the mud if they invaded Poland; Haushofer assured Hitler that it would not rain and that Poland would fall within eighteen days. The same year saw the generals urging an immediate invasion of France; Haushofer advised Hitler to wait until German propaganda had spread a defeatist mood among the French people. The generals advised against invading Norway; Haushofer assured Hitler that Germany would have an easy victory.

Haushofer used some strange turns of phrase when recommending his geopolitical thinking to others. His use of expressions such as 'the almost telepathic sensitivity of oceanic nations to foreign dangers'; and 'the demoniac beauty of geopolitics' led to many observers dismissing him as a crank or as someone who had perpetrated 'one of history's greatest hoaxes'. More informed observers felt very differently and as Hans Weigert wrote in July 1942:

> The highest eulogy a political writer could earn was to be called 'the American Haushofer'. Colleges all over the country [the USA] hurried to organize 'institutes of geopolitics'.

PHYSIOGNOMY AND PHRENOLOGY

For all their inherent absurdity it is possible to understand how and why race science and geopolitics could be pressed into the service of a totalitarian regime. It is much harder to see why so many other pseudo-sciences enjoyed toleration or even patronage in Nazi Germany. It was probably the relative ease with which they could be at least superficially assimilated to 'race science' that led to the revival and toleration of physiognomy and phrenology. Physiognomy is not as wholly irrational as most of the pseudo-sciences that found favour under the Nazis. It is the alleged ability to determine character from facial shape and expressions along with bodily gestures and is an essentially intuitive process. The eighteenth century saw an attempt by the Swiss writer Johann Kaspar Lavater to turn it into a rigid system. For a time he was considered the leading authority on the subject, but as time passed, his attempts to assign significance to every feature of the face and every bodily gesture became so difficult to reconcile with reality that they fell out of favour, before being taken up by Himmler and taught to the members of the SS as 'tests' for 'racial superiority'.

The same was true of phrenology, which was a 'science' without any kind of validity. It claimed to derive 'character' and 'aptitude' on the basis of bumps upon the head, and each bump was alleged to determine a particular attribute. Even the phrenologists could not agree on exactly how many bumps there were, with estimates ranging from thirty-three to thirty-seven and even forty. None of these assertions rested upon any evidence and before long phrenology was relegated to the occult underground. There it was found by Himmler who revived it and taught its 'principles' to the SS.

THE WORLD ICE THEORY

An extremely influential pseudo-scientific doctrine to which Hitler, Himmler, Rosenberg and others subscribed was the 'Glacial Cosmogony' of Hanns Hörbiger. This was also known as the *Welteislehre* (World Ice Theory), which in essence asserted that the universe represented an

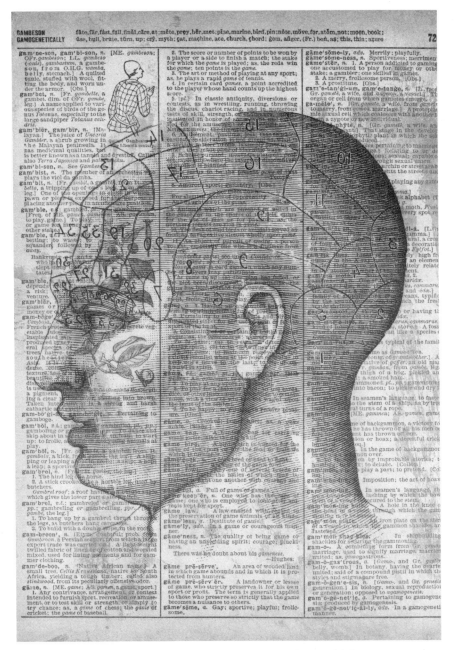

The Nazis found phrenology useful to their purposes – they could denounce an entire race as inferior due to the measurements taken from a tiny sample of citizens.

eternal struggle between fire and ice. It also claimed that the moon was a solid piece of ice that was not a native of the solar system but had been captured by earth's orbit around 11000BC. Hörbiger declared that there had been at least one previous moon which had collapsed on to the planet. According to Hörbiger's theory the 'capture' of earth's present moon led to the phenomenon described in the Bible as 'giants in those days'. He blamed the collapse of its predecessor for the destruction of Atlantis and the Great Flood.

Hörbiger arrived at his Glacial Cosmogony while working as an engineer. He saw molten steel being poured on to snow and the ground beneath erupting into a violent explosion. In that moment he became convinced that the universe had arisen through a similar process of cosmic ice being exposed to intense heat.

His theory declared that a huge particle of ice had collided with the sun and that this had resulted in an explosion whose after-effects were still continuing. The Flood, Atlantis, the Ice Age and similar events in the history of the earth all stemmed ultimately from that primordial collision between fire and ice. Even the different ethnic types on earth had arisen as a result of these cataclysmic events.

ATLANTIS AND GLACIAL COSMOGONY

German Atlantologists were increasingly prone to associate the fall of Atlantis with Hörbiger's theory but non-Germans also began to adopt it. In Britain the Druid Lewis Spence at least considered it possible though unlikely and Hans Bellamy and Peter Allan adopted the belief wholesale. They wrote a series of books advocating Hörbiger's Glacial Cosmogony.

Hörbiger and his disciples believed that the collapse of the earth's previous moon led to the melting of the glaciers and a consequent vast deluge that overwhelmed Atlantis with the vast tsunami that followed. The Ice Age had destroyed Aryan Atlantis, the greatest civilization ever seen on earth. Modern humans were only slowly beginning to approach the lost splendour of that sunken continent.

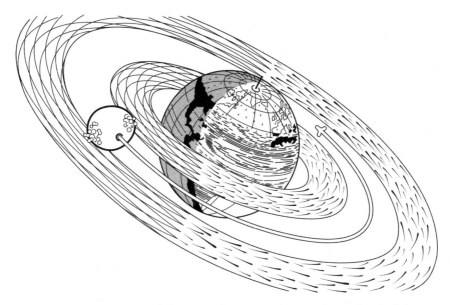

Hörbiger's Ice Theory found favour with Hans Robert Scultetus, head of the SS-Ahnenerbe metereology section, who believed it would provide long-term weather forecast.

Hitler often expressed his belief in the World Ice Theory and Himmler not only believed in it but propagandized extensively on its behalf. Himmler asked Kiss on his visit to Ethiopia to investigate any traces of cosmic ice as well as searching for the Ark of the Covenant. He set up a department within the *Ahnenerbe* dedicated to predicting the weather on the basis of the Cosmic Ice Theory. Himmler suppressed public criticism of Hörbiger's ideas and deluged other Nazi leaders with literature on the subject. He ordered the German mountaineers climbing Nanga Parbat to carry out experiments to demonstrate the truth of the theory. In 1937 a handbook on cosmic ice was produced and distributed to senior SA leaders. It included the notorious words 'the theory of relativity is to it [Hörbiger's Glacial Cosmogony] as the Talmud to the Edda'. Hitler was so impressed with the World Ice Theory that he compared Hörbiger with Copernicus and declared in 1942 that when the war was over he would build an observatory in Linz dedicated to him.

This theory had disastrous practical consequences for the Nazis. In 1941 the Hörbigerian 'weather forecasters' promised a mild winter which meant that the German troops invading the Soviet Union were not equipped with winter clothing, a fundamental error that cost many lives needlessly. Later in the war the Germans periodically halted work on their rocket programmes because Hörbiger's followers were anxious about upsetting 'the delicate balance between fire and ice'.

Glacial Cosmogony brought no benefit at all to the Nazis, but large sums of public money were squandered upon it. It also decisively affected the course of the war in a wholly negative way. It is incredible that a modern technological state like Germany with its fine tradition in science could have been so mesmerized by the theory that it allowed its notions to influence key military decisions.

THE HOLLOW EARTH THEORY

An even more absurd pseudo-scientific theory was strongly supported by both Goering and the German Navy. This was the idea that the earth

In 1941, Hörbigerian 'weather forecasters' promised a mild winter which meant that German troops invading the Soviet Union were not equipped with winter clothing.

was hollow and humans lived inside it, with a 'phantom universe', at the extremities of the earth. The North and South Poles were believed to be 'openings' to a subterranean world. This fantasy tied in well with the occult notions of the members of the Vril Society and other leading Nazis.

Money was actually wasted on two experiments designed to prove the truth of the hollow earth theory. The first was known as the Magdeburg Project and involved several test launches of rockets. The theory was that if the rockets crashed on the other side of the globe that would 'prove' that the earth was hollow.

Successive tests resulted in a complete failure to launch, with the rockets crashing soon after release or flying off and their subsequent whereabouts being unknown.

Even this series of expensive failures did not deter Goering and the navy from continuing to pursue 'research' into this idea. The logic behind this futile endeavour was to try and locate the British fleet.

In 1942 they sent a ten-man party under the leadership of an expert in infrared rays from Berlin to the island of Rügen. The theory was that the hollow earth's curvature would enable them to photograph the British fleet if the pictures were taken at an angle of forty-five degrees.

Naturally this experiment also failed and this time Hitler lost patience. Rosenberg had already denounced the hollow earth theory as 'a completely unscientific explanation of outer space' and not even Goering's advocacy could prevent the theory from being banned and its supporters thrown into concentration camps.

ARYAN PHYSICS

Less wholly irrational than the Cosmic Ice and hollow earth theories was the idea of 'Aryan physics'. Unlike the cranks and charlatans who argued in favour of the former notions, the supporters of Aryan physics at least included some first-rate scientific brains.

The idea of Aryan physics first arose during the First World War. It centred on the rejection of the theory of relativity and in many cases of quantum physics as well. Aryan physicists argued that both theories had not been proved and that other explanations were available along the lines of the classical principles of Newton.

The two leading exponents of Aryan physics were Philipp Lenard and Johannes Stark. Both men were brilliant scientists and many of their criticisms of the new ideas in physics were cogent. However they maintained their opposition in the face of increasing evidence that they were wrong and their doubts hardened into dogma.

Some Aryan physicists were willing to accept quantum physics and even some of the elements upon which relativity was based but refused to go along with relativity as a whole. The leading exponent of this partial accommodation between the old and new physics was Rudolf Tomaschek. He believed that the measurements of the orbit of Mercury and Arthur Eddington's eclipse experiments, which purportedly confirmed Einstein's theory, proved nothing and were capable of alternative explanations. Tomaschek also tried to ignore Einstein's work completely and proposed different interpretations of the scientific problems that had led to the creation of relativity theory.

Stark was a brilliant if old-fashioned physicist and although he was always an extreme German nationalist, his anti-Semitism appears to have arisen for personal reasons. As early as 1915 he clashed with a rival physicist, Arnold Sommerfeld, after the latter's pupil received a professorship which Stark had been seeking. He immediately claimed that 'Jewish and pro-Semitic circles' headed by Sommerfeld had intrigued against him to prevent his appointment.

In 1920 Stark was awarded the Nobel Prize for Physics and used the enhanced prestige that it gave him to begin his campaign against what he referred to as 'modern physics'. Stark's anti-Semitism was never ideological but remained a personal vendetta against scientists with whom he disagreed. He often avoided criticizing Jewish scientists and his most vitriolic attacks were generally reserved for 'Aryan' supporters of Einstein.

The first real attempt to create a movement that foreshadowed Aryan physics occurred in 1920 with a series of lectures in Berlin that denounced relativity. Einstein responded in a Berlin newspaper article where he accused his opponents of anti-Semitism and also criticized Lenard publicly. This was not only unwise but also unfair as Lenard had never previously attacked Einstein personally nor made any anti-Semitic remarks and had not even attended the Berlin lectures.

The result was a bitter personal animosity and the beginning of anti-Semitic attacks by Lenard on both Einstein and other supporters of relativity. When Einstein received his Nobel Prize in 1922, Stark and Lenard were outraged. That year, Stark published *The Contemporary Crisis in German Physics* in which he attacked both relativity and quantum physics as 'dogmatic'. He also complained that Einstein tried to popularize his theories through talks and newspaper articles rather than through scholarly work in the scientific community.

Although Lenard became a fanatical anti-Semite, Stark's own attitudes were more opportunistic and largely motivated by personal malice. He began to accuse any scientist who disagreed with him of either being Jewish or being a 'white Jew'. In 1923 he publicly supported the Nazis and visited Hitler during his imprisonment.

Lenard joined the Nazi Party during its early years and began to denounce relativity as 'Jewish physics'. When the Nazis came to power he and his ally Stark saw the chance to impose their views on the scientific community as a whole. Stark angled for the post of 'Führer of physics' and both men actively co-operated in the disgraceful purge of Jewish scientists. By 1937 they had succeeded in driving every one of them out of their positions.

Even with the Nazis in power Lenard and Stark faced opposition. Max Planck successfully manoeuvred to present an apparent conformity with 'German physics' and 'National Socialist principles' but in practice worked hard to preserve the integrity of German science. He could do nothing to prevent the dismissal of Jewish scientists from their positions but succeeded in ensuring that relativity and quantum physics remained an integral part of science in Germany. Max von Laue was a personal friend of Einstein's and gave a presentation on his theory in

January 1935. In April 1936 he delivered another on quantum theory. In spite of the fact that both relativity and quantum physics were being denounced by Stark and Lenard as 'Jewish physics', not a word of censure for von Laue followed.

Stark and Lenard were far less successful when they attacked 'Aryan' supporters of relativity. Walther Bothe openly supported Einstein's theories and though he was dismissed from his position at a state university the powerful patronage of Planck enabled him to continue his researches in the private sector.

When Stark and Lenard attacked Werner Heisenberg as a 'white Jew', they stirred up a hornets' nest. Heisenberg had gone to school with Himmler and after his mother protested to Himmler's mother about his harassment it abruptly stopped. In fact the result was that Lenard and Stark lost influence and Aryan physics began to fall out of favour. Himmler told Heisenberg that after the war he would be put in overall charge of German physics. Soon other scientists began to defend relativity and quantum physics and with the advent of war it was not Stark and Lenard but Bothe and Heisenberg and other supporters of Einstein who found themselves working for the German government to help win the war. Aryan physics was quietly pushed aside in the interests of victory.

GERMAN MATHEMATICS

As well as 'Aryan physics' there was a parallel movement known as *Deutsche Mathematik* (German mathematics) which was as viciously anti-Semitic as the physicists but had much less excuse for its attacks. There were at least genuine problems with the theory of relativity and even quantum physics. Mathematics was an entirely different matter.

The leading advocate of 'German mathematics' was Ludwig Bieberbach, a respected mathematician who had never shown any signs of Nazi sympathies before 1933. His 'conversion' to a National Socialist 'attitude' was purely opportunistic and he only began advocating his theories on 'German mathematics' after 1933.

Bieberbach put forward the idea that because of the ethnic differences between Aryans and Jews they created entirely different types of mathematics because of their 'psychological natures', which derived from their dissimilar 'racial origins'. This self-evident nonsense would have been laughed at in any other society but because of the obsessional anti-Semitism in Nazi Germany his work was praised.

Just as Stark tried to make himself the scientific dictator of Germany, so Bieberbach aspired to become the *Führer* of German mathematics. His attempts to seize control of mathematical activity within the country failed, but his campaign to expel Jews from positions in the field was more successful.

THE CAMPAIGN AGAINST JEWISH SCIENTISTS

From 30 September 1933, German scientific and mathematical organizations were required to ensure that foreign corresponding members were 'racially pure' and not 'politically objectionable'. This idea had been proposed by Bieberbach and was adopted by the German Ministry of Education. In 1936 Bieberbach tried to impose Nazi candidates upon the Prussian Academy of Sciences (PAW) but was unsuccessful.

The PAW continued to have Jews among its membership and in January 1937 it was openly attacked for allowing them to belong, as well as being accused of hostility towards National Socialism.

In February 1937 it was required to give an account of how many 'non-Aryan' members it had and in particular how many were Jewish.

On 1 March 1937 the PAW responded to the 'request'. Among the society's members there were three non-Aryans and one who was a quarter Jewish. None of the society's German corresponding members were Jewish but they were unable to provide information about foreign members. In April their report openly expressed their concern that expelling all Jewish members would lead to mass resignations from the academy by its foreign members. Bieberbach refused to sign this document but the Ministry of Education was more flexible. By a process of slow attrition the remaining Jewish members were forced out during the course of the year. It was a sad chapter in the history of German science and mathematics.

VIKTOR SCHAUBERGER AND LIVING WATER

The final area of irrational and pseudo-scientific beliefs to have influence within Nazi Germany was represented by the ideas of the Austrian Viktor Schauberger. His whole conception of science was rooted in occultism and it is no surprise that he attracted the attention of Himmler and ultimately Hitler. Schauberger was a forester by trade and many of his concerns about deforestation and the water table were justified. However he expressed his views in the context of an entirely nebulous mysticism and denied that the chemical formula H_2O represented 'real' water. He described it as 'sterile water' and contrasted it with the properties of what he called 'living water'. Schauberger described water as the 'blood of Mother Earth' which was 'born' in the forests. What we think of as water, he declared, was only 'juvenile water' without any properties of its own. Only as it absorbs minerals, salts and even odours from everything it passes through or has contact with and becomes enriched by them does water have value, he believed.

Schauberger considered that sunlight was harmful to water and that its quality was at its greatest if it flowed in darkness or at least in shade. He evolved the theory that the flow of water was regulated by 'natural vortices'. Schauberger claimed that by using this principle he could create a 'centrifugal movement' that overrode Archimedes' theories on the displacement of water. He took out a number of patents for an 'air turbine', a 'procedure for lifting liquid and gases' and a 'warm-cold machine' from 1929 onwards.

In 1934 Schauberger met Hitler and discussed forestry, agriculture and water management. Nothing seems to have come of this meeting but following the *Anschluss* with Austria in 1938 Himmler immediately demanded that Schauberger began working on behalf of the SS. In 1940 he developed and took out patents for the Repulsin discoid motor. Not long after, he was arrested by the SS and detained in a mental hospital. On his release, he worked with the Messerschmitt aircraft company on a liquid vortex cooling system. The rival Heinkel firm also recruited him to work on cooling aircraft engines and to see if his Repulsin discoid motor could be developed for use in planes.

The Heinkel design was for a cigar-shaped aircraft. Himmler ordered Schauberger to work at Mauthausen concentration camp and he was placed in charge of around thirty inmates who were engineers. His research was described as being concerned with 'higher atomic energies'. The team worked hard to build a prototype that was eventually tested in a laboratory. The Repulsin A rose swiftly in a vertical take-off before smashing to pieces on the ceiling. Schauberger was accused of sabotage but was allowed to continue work on an improved version of his idea.

He was next ordered to work on fitting the Repulsin B motor to an advanced type of submarine known as the Forelle (trout) because of its unusual shape, which resembled a fish with its mouth open. By 1944 the SS had abandoned this particular idea but ordered Schauberger to apply the Repulsin B instead to experimental flying disc aircraft. Schauberger had developed a type of turbine that created an upward vortex of air that was able to power the machine through drag and 'moving air'. It flew successfully in 1944 but nothing more is known about any wartime developments of the model. The overall development of his Repulsins continued until May 1945. That year he also began work upon the Klimator, a device to heat and cool air.

Following the defeat of Germany Schauberger was arrested by the US and all of his models and research notes were seized by them. He remained under arrest for the next nine months.

The basis upon which Schauberger's machines operated remains a secret as all his work passed into the hands of intelligence agencies. Clues exist within his writing and the most relevant quotation has led to claims that he developed a form of 'free energy' or 'perpetual motion' machine.

If water or air is rotated into a twisting form of oscillation known as 'colloidal', a build up of energy results, which, with immense power, can cause levitation. This form of movement is able to carry with it its own means of power generation. This principle leads logically to its application in the design of the ideal airplane or submarine requiring almost no motive power.

Schauberger also claimed that nature possessed 'growing and increasing reserves of energy' which in his view 'results first and foremost in the collapse of the so-called Law of the Conservation of Energy, and in further consequence the Law of Gravity'.

Comments of that nature certainly place Schauberger firmly in the same irrational and occult universe that Himmler inhabited. His obsession with the notion that every aspect of nature was a living presence and that such established principles as gravity and the conservation of energy were false makes Schauberger's ideas firmly the product of mysticism rather than of science. His work on anti-gravity research produced little significant progress and it is entirely characteristic of the Nazi regime that it preferred to devote money, time and resources towards work that was at best of only marginal and long-term significance rather than upon research that might actually have influenced the course of the war in its favour.

Chapter Ten
OCCULTISM AT WAR

AT THE DARK HEART of the Nazis' vision lay such a fundamental inversion of most accepted moral and spiritual values that they aroused fierce opposition even before they came to power. The campaign to control occult activity within Germany began in 1933 and was more or less complete by 1937. Following the flight of Hess to Britain in 1941, the few remaining independent occultists within the Reich were rounded up and thrown into concentration camps.

The coming of war in 1939 saw a ferocious military, political and economic struggle being fought across Europe. As well as the 'public' face of the war a 'psychic conflict' also took place which was fought at the highest level. Inside Germany few were either capable or courageous enough to join the anti-Nazi spiritual conflict directly but a few did so. Britain needed all the help it could get and Churchill in particular encouraged the use of every possible method of psychological warfare.

THE 1939 ASSASSINATION ATTEMPT ON HITLER

The 1939 assassination attempt against Hitler had a number of occult elements. Many myths have grown up around this event in addition to downright fabrications and a large amount of deliberate disinformation on the part of two agents of British Intelligence.

The bare facts of the case are remarkable enough. A carpenter named Georg Elser decided to assassinate Hitler. He considered the best method of achieving his goal and settled on an explosive device at the annual celebration of the failed Munich Putsch on 8 November. Elser was a Communist but had never been a particularly active member of the party.

He simply made up his mind that Hitler had to be killed and that he knew how it could be done.

The occult associations with the plot begin with the Swiss astrologer Karl Krafft. He had been working on a freelance basis for Heinrich Fesel of the Gestapo since 1933. In spite of his Swiss origins, Krafft had fallen out with his native country and had moved to Germany in 1936. He became a convinced Nazi and Fesel placed him on the Gestapo payroll, probably more in the hope that he might be useful at some point in the future than from any particular purpose for which he considered his occult talents might be used. Krafft drew up horoscopes of Chamberlain, Roosevelt, Churchill and other Western politicians to make astrological predictions about their future.

Krafft is primarily remembered as an astrologer but he was one of the leading experts on the interpretation of the prophecies of Nostradamus and he also invented a mumbo-jumbo theory of linguistics known as *Sprachgeist* ('the spirit of language') as well as developing a new approach to astrology which he called astro-biology. Through Fesel he met the senior Nazi leaders Robert Ley and Hans Frank and began to hope that he might be recruited for more important work on behalf of the regime.

His 'forecast' on 2 November 1939 was startlingly specific. His latest astrological prediction to Fesel declared that between 8 and 9 November Hitler's life would be in danger from 'an attempt of assassination by the use of explosive material'. Fesel did not pass on this particular forecast to his superior and no doubt considered it yet another crank prediction.

On the evening of 8 November Hitler gave his annual speech at the Party meeting in memory of the failed Munich Putsch. A bomb exploded in the hall and seven Nazis were killed and many more injured. Hitler had spoken for nearly an hour before leaving and only missed being assassinated by fifteen minutes. Fesel was already nervous about not having passed on the warning but Krafft, who clearly had megalomaniac tendencies, sent a telegram to Hess boasting about his prediction.

It remains a mystery why he chose to contact Hess, a man whom he had never met, rather than Ley or Hans Frank whom he did at least know slightly. Probably the most logical person for him to have contacted was his existing Gestapo contact Fesel. Krafft was also clearly not living in the real world or the last thing he would have done on any rational assessment of the situation was to claim foreknowledge of an attempt on Hitler's life.

Naturally the Gestapo arrested him and Fesel hastily produced Krafft's prediction. The astrologer was grilled relentlessly but was eventually able to persuade them that he had only known about the plot through his study of the stars.

Krafft now came to the attention of Himmler and Goebbels, both of whom decided that he could be a useful tool. In early 1938 he told the Romanian ambassador that the fascist politician Codreanu would die in November of that year and that the King of Romania would lose his power. Both predictions came true and were largely responsible for the subsequent wartime career of Louis de Wohl.

Himmler was primarily interested in Krafft's astrological skills; Goebbels was impressed by his knowledge of Nostradamus and immediately recruited him to the Propaganda Ministry. In early 1940 Krafft was asked to produce a new 'edition' of the French prophet's work while inserting a number of forged prophecies within it predicting a German victory in the war.

The Bürgerbräukeller in Munich after the explosion which nearly claimed Hitler's life in 1939: Hitler missed assassination by 15 minutes after he left the premises earlier than he was supposed to.

Krafft actually wrote a number of fake Nostradamus prophecies which the Germans circulated within France. They proved surprisingly effective as propaganda weapons and helped to spread a spirit of defeatism among the French and to lower their morale.

BRITISH BLACK OPERATIONS AND DIRTY TRICKS

These actions on the Nazis' part led to the decision by British Intelligence to retaliate in kind. From the very beginning of the war the Special Operations Executive (SOE) had been working on a campaign of 'dirty tricks' against the Germans and the Hungarian exile Louis de Wohl was recruited by them to work on 'occult propaganda' stunts. De Wohl wrote articles for fake editions of *Zenit*, Hubert Korsch's astrological magazine – though the British made the mistake of calling their version

Der Zenit – as well as forging Nostradamus prophecies of his own. Although de Wohl exaggerated both his own importance and that of Krafft, he certainly did work on black ops for Sefton Delmer's 'black ops' team and his activities probably helped raise morale at home and lower it abroad, if only slightly.

Before turning to de Wohl's colourful career a word must be said about Delmer and his extraordinarily successful use of black propaganda. At several key points in the war his work actually affected its outcome decisively.

From 1939, SOE was in charge of propaganda and disinformation. In 1941 the Psychological Warfare Executive was set up as a separate department and Delmer was placed in effective charge. His brief was psychological warfare and dirty tricks and while much of his department's work was 'white' propaganda through broadcasts to Europe from the BBC and official British government leaflets dropped over enemy territory by the RAF it also had a darker side. 'Black' operations were designed to mislead and to disguise their British origin and give the impression that they were official German broadcasts or publications.

It was not until 1941 that Delmer's black ops came fully into operation. On 23 May 1941 the *Gustaf Siegfried Eins* radio station (GS1) began broadcasting and in November 1941 the printing and distribution of fake leaflets began. Much of the material produced by Delmer's team was straightforward propaganda but a surprisingly large amount of it involved the occult.

GS1 was a remarkably successful exercise in black propaganda. It featured a supposed Nazi called 'Der Chef' who lambasted Churchill and what he called 'Party Communists', whom he accused of betraying the Nazi revolution. Sir Stafford Cripps was so appalled by Delmer's propaganda that he told Anthony Eden, the Foreign Secretary, 'If this is the sort of thing that is needed to win the war, why, I'd rather lose it.' Fortunately both Eden and Churchill disagreed and Delmer's operations expanded.

ASTROLOGICAL WARFARE

As early as spring 1940 'astrological warfare' was being used by the Germans, mainly on the basis of horoscope interpretations drawn up by Krafft. By the summer of that year the British decided to counter this with propaganda of their own and de Wohl was recommended for the job by the Romanian ambassador. He met Lord Halifax and was soon asked to begin working for British Intelligence, initially on a freelance basis but eventually in an official capacity.

By December 1940, the first edition of Krafft's version of the prophecies of Nostradamus appeared. It was a highly selective reading of the sixteenth-century French prophet's work with an extensive commentary by Krafft and a number of forged prophecies. The entire work was presented with a pro-Nazi slant and promised a swift German victory in the war.

Although the first book-length Nostradamus forgery did not appear until the end of 1940, as early as May of that year leaflets containing selected prophecies with interpretations, some genuine but slanted, others outright forgeries, were circulated in Holland, Belgium and France. They helped to foster a defeatist mood among the people and government and were one of the most spectacularly successful examples of German wartime propaganda.

Across the Channel the British were thinking along similar lines. A particular area of concern was the growing success of the German propaganda machine in its task of planting articles and letters in American astrological publications, predicting a German victory in the war. De Wohl was sent to America by the SOE in May 1941 to counter this strategy with astrological predictions of his own, which announced imminent disaster in Germany. He was remarkably successful in raising public support for Britain and turning American public opinion against the Nazis. His own forged Nostradamus prophecies also helped to sow doubt about the regime in the minds of ordinary Germans, particularly after the invasion of the Soviet Union began to falter.

Hitler tightly controlled occult activity within the Reich and suppressed many organizations that were sympathetic towards the Nazis, as well as outright opponents. Even so, the influence upon the *Führer* and other leading Nazis of the intellectual underworld they inhabited remained marked, in spite of the fact that much of this activity had been driven underground.

Although the official attitude towards the occult was one of disapproval there was a rush to 'integrate' its practitioners within the framework of the state and the Nazi Party. Before long most of those who continued to practise found themselves working for the Third Reich.

Some of the pro-Nazi or at least fellow-traveller groups to fall out of favour included the *Mazdaznan* cult, whose members combined elements of the Zoroastrian religion with vegetarianism, an obsession with constipation and a belief that only light-skinned Aryans could be 'saved'. Many adherents of the order had been strong supporters of Hitler and were astonished when the regime suppressed them.

CROWLEY'S *BOOK OF THE LAW* AND HITLER

Another group that fell foul of the Nazis was the Ordo Templi Orientis (O.T.O.), Aleister Crowley's 'magical' order. This used 'sex magic' as a way of 'achieving enlightenment' and one of its leading German members was strongly pro-Nazi. There are various stories concerning this woman's alleged influence upon Hitler but none seem particularly plausible.

It is certain that in 1925 Crowley told Marthe Künzel, head of the German branch of the O.T.O., that the first country to adopt his *Book of the Law* as its sacred text would become the most powerful nation in the world. Künzel is alleged to have been a friend of Rudolf Hess and to have aroused his interest in Crowley's work. Another story claims that Künzel carried out a ritual after which she believed that Hitler was her 'magical child'. It was said that she also presented Hitler with a copy of the *Book of the Law* in 1926 or 1927.

It is not impossible that Hess and Künzel might have been friends. Nor is there anything improbable in the idea of Hess reading the *Book of the Law*. He was perhaps the most occultly inclined of all the Nazis leaders, even Himmler, and would probably have read Crowley's work with interest. Further than that it is impossible to determine any direct influence by Künzel or Crowley upon Hess.

Hitler is a different matter and one where there clearly does seem to be at least the possibility of some kind of direct influence. Crowley and Hitler never met and even the man christened by the tabloid press as 'the wickedest man in the world' decided that Hitler had become a 'black brother'. We know that Künzel was an admirer of Hitler and a strong supporter of the Nazis and that she met with the *Führer* on a number of occasions. As the leading exponent of Crowley's ideas in Germany it is highly likely that she would have presented Hitler with a copy of the *Book of the Law* and urged him to adopt it as his 'testament'.

Hitler had no intention of allowing any 'sacred book' to govern his ideas and actions but there are certainly close enough parallels between some aspects of Crowley's thought and even paraphrases of the book to suggest that Hitler did at least read the *Book of the Law*. When war broke out in 1939, Crowley wrote to Künzel and told her that Britain would 'knock Hitler for a six'. Künzel also wrote to Crowley earlier that year and declared:

> It began to dawn upon me how many of Hitler's thoughts were as if they had been taken from the law of Thelema [Crowley's philosophy]. I became his fervent admirer, and am so now, and will be to my end. The close identity of Hitler's ideas with what the Book [Book of the Law] teaches endowed me with the strength necessary for my work. I stated this even to the Gestapo some years ago.

There is no doubt, then, that Künzel was both a Nazi and a disciple of Crowley and that she also presented Hitler with a copy of the *Book of the Law*. A number of quotes from Hitler show signs that some of its wilder

Aleister Crowley told Marthe Künzel, head of the German branch of the Ordo Templis Orientis, that the first country to adopt his Book of the Law *as its sacred text would become the most powerful nation on earth.*

ramblings at least struck a chord with the German dictator. Apart from that it is unsafe to make further deductions about possible influence.

CROWLEY AND BRITISH INTELLIGENCE

With the outbreak of war Crowley, like other British occultists, wanted to assist in the war effort. He was invited to visit the Director of Naval Intelligence and claimed that as a result of their meeting two 'magical signs' were adopted at his suggestion. The famous 'V-sign' used by Churchill was said to be the 'magical counter' to the reversed swastika and the 'thumbs up' sign was allegedly a symbol of victory and sexual magic.

Partly because of Crowley's flamboyant, disreputable and vain-glorious nature, doubt has been cast upon his claims. These suspicions are entirely understandable but as with the story about Künzel and Hitler there is a certain amount of fire behind the smoke. Crowley certainly was invited to meet the Director of Naval Intelligence and although we only have his word as to what took place at that meeting, it is not at all implausible. To claim the authorship of two symbols is, by the standards of Crowley's outsized ego, a very mild and minor example of arrogance that might well be true.

CHURCHILL THE DRUID

Churchill was in charge of the navy at that time and a man as anti-establishment, humorous and imaginative as him may well have considered it at least worth investigating any ideas Crowley might have had. Apart from the fact that he placed great emphasis on psychological and even psychic warfare, especially once he became Prime Minister, Churchill was also a man far more interested in, and even involved with, occultism than is generally realized. Churchill was a Druid who was initiated into the Albion Lodge of the Ancient Order of Druids at Blenheim on 15 April 1908. According to Dennis Wheatley (who worked for British Intelligence during the war) he was also a member of the Illuminati, perhaps the most famous secret society of all time. Churchill certainly recruited a number of occultists to assist the war effort and placed many of them on the government payroll. The majority of them found themselves working for Sefton Delmer's 'black ops' section of British Intelligence, which was designed to spread disinformation and a spirit of defeatism among the German people.

THE MAGICAL BATTLE OF BRITAIN

The so-called 'magical Battle of Britain' predated the physical conflict by a considerable time and also continued after the heroism of the RAF's pilots had won the aerial duel with the Luftwaffe. Many occultists became involved in this psychic warfare but perhaps the most continuously active figure in this area of conflict was Dion Fortune. On the outbreak of war, she mobilized her order, the Fraternity of the Inner Light, to take up the 'magical defence of the realm'.

Fortune set up her 'occult headquarters' in London although another property in Glastonbury also became involved. From October 1939 to October 1942, she persuaded large numbers of her followers and others involved in the occult or psychic fields to conduct weekly rituals designed to create a shield of protection over Britain.

She sent out a series of letters, weekly at first but on a monthly basis once the tide of the war had begun to turn in favour of the Allies. In these letters she instructed people to perform various 'magical' meditations between 12.15 and 12.30 every Sunday afternoon. She told those who took part in these meditative sessions that they should:

Take your seat if possible in a quiet, dimly lit room secure from disturbance; face toward London; sit in an attitude that your feet are together and your hands clasped, thus making a closed circuit of yourself. Your hands should rest on the weekly letter lying on your lap.

Fortune saw herself, her order and those who joined in her meditations as engaged in 'a true crusade against the powers of darkness'. She believed that Britain was under the 'magical protection' of Arthur and his knights. Glastonbury was in her eyes the 'sacred centre' of Britain and the focus of many of her meditations. She urged people to

think of yourself as part of the Group-soul of your race; your life a part of its life, and its life the basis of yours. Then, invoking the name of God, open your mind as a channel for the work of the Masters of Wisdom.

On 28 February 1940 Fortune told her followers to 'meditate upon angelic presences' who were 'moving as a vast shadowy power across the coasts' to make sure that 'nothing alien can move unobserved'. On 21 April 1940 Fortune asked her co-meditators to patrol the 'North Sea coastline' and even 'to carry the patrol through the narrow waters into the Baltic'. Before long she encouraged her followers to engage in 'magical attacks' on the 'astral plane'. They were directed to imagine themselves carrying fiery torches and swords aimed in the direction of Germany. She demanded that they should enter the offices and bedrooms of Nazi leaders and try to divert their behaviour into the service of good rather than evil.

Fortune was convinced that the Nazis were also actively engaged in a psychic campaign against Britain. She wrote:

We are dealing with definite occult forces being used telepathically on the group souls of nations, and finding channels of expression through the subconscious of susceptible people who lack spiritual principles.

Fortune believed that this alleged activity was widespread and declared that 'so specialised and unrecognised is it that we might justly talk of sixth column activities'. Curiously enough in spite of the large amount of time and money wasted by the Germans on occult activities there is little or no evidence that such 'magical duelling' was practised by Nazi occultists. Fortune's activities probably helped raise morale among those who took part but it is doubtful whether they made any difference to the course of the war.

THE DRUIDS AND PSYCHIC WARFARE

Fortune's Fraternity of the Inner Light was not the only group to become involved in attempts at psychic warfare. The Druids also held ceremonies, with the two most important ones being in Wales and the Isle of Man. On Lammas Eve (31 July 1940) a group of Druids performed a ritual to keep the Nazis at bay. They visualized a shield of protection all round the British Isles and projected 'rays of power' to turn back the enemy. The Druids also turned their psychic energies into launching these rays against the invasion barges as well as trying to hypnotically suggest to their crew that they needed to retreat and that their planned invasion was doomed to failure. Later in the year a similar ceremony held at Halloween reinforced the message of the utter impossibility of an invasion. The Druids summoned to their assistance all the spirits of water, earth, air and fire and believed that by joining natural energy forces to their own human wills their ceremonies would become infinitely more powerful.

The Scottish Druid Lewis Spence became actively involved in conspiracies against Hitler within Germany. The common link between him and the German anti-Nazis he contacted was Hörbiger's Glacial Cosmogony theory. Both Spence and his fellow occultist Egerton Sykes wrote extensively on the subject of Atlantis and Spence also produced a number of works on Druidism.

The Hörbiger Institute in Vienna was run by Hörbiger's three sons, Hanns Robert, Hans and Alfred with the assistance of the secretary Georg Hinzpeter. Hinzpeter was not an admirer of the Nazis and neither was Hanns Robert. This particular Hörbiger belonged to a Druid order through which he and Spence shared ideas. Spence was never convinced by Hörbiger's theories but Sykes undoubtedly found them persuasive. He remained in contact with Hinzpeter throughout the war.

The Hörbiger Institute in Vienna clashed constantly with the Nazi authorities from the time of the *Anschluss* in 1938 to its eventual closure in 1942. Curiously the Nazis accused it of 'high treason' for continuing to publish its proceedings and compelled it to close altogether. For the last three years of the war the Institute became an engineering factory.

Although contact between Spence and Sykes on the one hand and Hinzpeter and Hanns Robert Hörbiger on the other is certain, no details have emerged of the precise nature or results of these exchanges. An intriguing possibility is that the Hörbigerian weather forecasts for the Russian winter in 1941 may have been faked as an act of deliberate sabotage. Beyond that possibility we can only speculate. Both Hess and Spence were interested in the Rosicrucians, an alleged secret society that arose around the beginning of the seventeenth century. Spence specifically linked Rosicrucianism with the Grail legends and also with Druidism.

He also claimed that the Nazis had been infiltrated by occult groups that represented 'a new and particularly abandoned agency for the dissemination of the cult of Satanism'. Spence believed that these underground organizations had been founded 'for the express purpose of functioning in the event of the defeat of the Nazi Party' and that they had also infiltrated the secret Communist network in Germany. These occultists were allegedly based primarily in Munich.

CEREMONIES BY BRITISH WITCHES

In 1940 another occult group became involved with magical workings in an attempt to repel the imminent threat of German invasion. A coven of witches in Hampshire decided to perform a ritual at the Rufus Stone in the New Forest. Through a mixture of chanting and dancing its members tried to block the German invaders. One of the members, Gerald Gardner, was later largely responsible for the revival of witchcraft in Britain. He wrote about the ceremony as follows:

> *The great cone of power was raised and slowly directed in the general direction of Hitler. The command was given: 'You cannot cross the sea, you cannot cross the sea, you cannot come, you cannot come.' Just as was done to Napoleon and the Spanish Armada.*

Seventeen witches were present at this ceremony, five of whom died shortly afterwards. As with Fortune's magical workings, the rituals probably helped to raise morale among people within the esoteric community.

Crowley is said to have been involved in two magical ceremonies. The first was dreamed up by Ian Fleming and its purpose was to lure Hess into defecting to Britain. Allegedly soldiers went to Ashdown Forest in Sussex during 1941 where Crowley burnt a dummy in Nazi uniform to the accompaniment of ritual chanting.

There are several different versions of this story, all contradictory as to time, location, numbers of people involved and even the nature of the ritual. As neither Fleming nor Crowley ever made any claim to have performed or even organized such an event it is almost certainly a later invention. Certainly the story was never mentioned before the 1990s, which casts further doubt on its authenticity. It is true that Fleming worked on plans to lure Hess to Britain through some sort of deliberate occult disinformation, but it is highly doubtful that Crowley played any part in these operations.

The same is true of another ceremony that Crowley is alleged to have carried out in 1943 at the Men an Tol megalithic site in Cornwall. This is alleged to have impacted on the Battle of the Atlantic and the Philadelphia Experiment (of which more will be heard shortly). Again there is no evidence for any such activity; Crowley never mentioned any such rituals; nor did the story emerge before the 1990s. Once more it seems an invention rather than sober fact.

HESS FLIES TO BRITAIN

One of the most baffling and controversial events of the Second World War took place on 10 May 1941. That day saw Rudolf Hess, the deputy *Führer*, take off from Germany in a custom-built Messerschmitt 110 long-range fighter aircraft. His plane included a hypodermic syringe, a large number of homeopathic medicines and visiting cards from both Karl Haushofer and his son Albrecht. Hess landed in Scotland and

The *Rufus Stone* in the New Forest, England marks the spot where William II was accidentally killed while hunting stags in AD1100; it was chosen by Gerald Gardner and other British witches to stage a magic ceremony against the Nazis in 1940.

attempted to contact the Duke of Hamilton to present peace proposals to the British government.

The reasons for his flight to Britain remain obscure. Theories range from the suggestion that deliberate disinformation from British Intelligence had lured him into a carefully prepared trap; that it was a cunning plan by Himmler, Heydrich or perhaps both to sow confusion in the British ranks and disguise the forthcoming invasion of Russia; that it was a plot conceived by Albrecht Haushofer to try and bring peace or perhaps overthrow Hitler; that Hess felt he was falling out of favour with Hitler and wanted to redeem himself by carrying out a spectacular mission; that Hess had acted as he did on the basis of astrological and occult advice; that he had simply suffered a nervous breakdown; or that he had defected to the British.

All of these theories have a certain degree of plausibility. There is no doubt that Hess became increasingly disillusioned with the regime after the *Kristallnacht* atrocities in 1938. British Intelligence certainly considered the idea of luring Hess to Britain and did make considerable use of forged astrological and occult material throughout the war. Himmler certainly appears to have been contemplating removing Hitler from power and taking over himself at about the period in question. The devious Heydrich was certainly capable of anything and his cunning made him perhaps the most dangerous of all the Nazi leaders. Albrecht Haushofer certainly became anti-Nazi later, but at this stage of the war both he and his father were close to Himmler and no signs of their later opposition to the regime had been displayed. There is little evidence that Hess had fallen out of favour and the idea that he would have undertaken such a risky mission without some reason for believing in its success seems highly improbable. Nor was Hess significantly odder in 1941 than he had been previously.

The true explanation is probably a combination of factors. Hess had always been a disciple of the senior Haushofer and had always believed that war with Britain was a mistake. Since the fall of France he had extended peace feelers through neutral countries and organizations and he had been learning to fly the Me-110 plane since September 1940.

In January 1941 the British used Carl Burckhardt of the Red Cross to relay a message to the Wednesday Society, a group of anti-Nazi conservative nationalists. Burckhardt told the group that the British government was prepared to make peace with Germany if Holland, Belgium and Poland were restored to their independence and Hitler stood down as Chancellor. Albrecht Haushofer was a member of this society and Burckhardt expressed a desire to meet with him.

Carl Langbehn, another member of the society but who was in reality a 'plant' by Himmler inside the opposition, asked Burckhardt to approach the British government and see if they would be willing to make peace with a Germany led by Himmler instead of Hitler. In April 1941 Albrecht Haushofer met Hess several times and on 28 April Haushofer travelled to Switzerland to meet Burckhardt on behalf of what appears to have been a joint peace initiative by Hess, Himmler and the Wednesday Society.

Hess was also told by Karl Haushofer that he had seen a vision of the deputy *Führer* striding through baronial halls and brokering peace between Britain and Germany. Albrecht Haushofer drew up a horoscope that predicted success for the mission and showed it to Hess. The result was his landing in Britain and his immediate arrest. Whatever the true reason for his flight to Britain it was a spectacular failure on every level.

What is certain is that when Hess flew to Britain Fleming approached his superiors in naval intelligence and suggested that Crowley would be the ideal person to debrief him. Crowley was enthusiastic about the idea and wrote to the Director of Naval Intelligence to offer his services, declaring that he believed he could persuade Hess to co-operate. Using Crowley's services may well have been considered but ultimately Fleming's plan was rejected.

NAZI CRACKDOWN ON OCCULTISM

From the point of view of the occult practitioners within the Reich, Hess's flight to Britain was probably a baffling mystery. However its consequences were extremely unfortunate for them. Bormann suggested to Hitler not only that Hess had gone mad but that his insanity had been brought on by undue influence from astrologers. At this meeting Himmler was remarkably quiet, probably because of his known predilection for astrology but Goebbels, always one of the more rational Nazi leaders, supported Bormann's suggestion and agreed with him that an immediate crackdown on astrology was necessary. How far this was motivated by genuinely rational motives and how far both men seized on the opportunity to provide yet another excuse for repression is open to question. For whatever reason the decision to suppress and control astrology and other types of occult activity was taken and the Gestapo began the work of investigating and arresting astrologers throughout the Reich.

On 14 May the *Völkischer Beobachter* used its columns to declare:

> As was well known in Party circles, Rudolf Hess was in poor health for many years and latterly had recourse to hypnotists, astrologers and so on. The extent to which these people are responsible for the mental confusion that led him to his present step has still to be clarified.

Curiously the very same day saw a strange article in *The Times* allegedly based upon information received from its Swiss correspondent. *The Times* announced:

> Certain of Hess' close friends have thrown an interesting light on the affair. They say that Hess has always been Hitler's astrologer in secret. Up to last March he had consistently predicted good fortune and had always been right. Since then, notwithstanding the victories Germany has won, he has declared that the stars showed that Hitler's meteoric career was approaching its climax.

There followed an order from Bormann on 6–7 June 1941 in which action against Christians, 'astrologers, fortune-tellers and other swindlers' was announced. On 24 June 1941 the Ministry of Propaganda banned public performances of anything, including demonstrations of telepathy, clairvoyance, astrology, spiritualism or other occult activities. On 30 October 1941 the publishing of articles on these subjects was forbidden.

On 9 June 1941 there ensued the bulk of the arrests in what became known as *Aktion-Hess*. The Gestapo arrested astrologers, palmists, graphologists, Christian Scientists, faith healers, psychologists and anthroposophists. Their net of suspects was extremely wide but most were released after three or four weeks of fairly intensive questioning. The most high profile individuals arrested at this time were Korsch and Krafft. Korsch was murdered in a concentration camp in 1942; Krafft suffered the same fate in 1944.

SOVIET PSYCHIC WARFARE

Perhaps surprisingly the Soviet Union, committed to atheism and an official belief in a purely physical explanation of the world, was at the forefront of paranormal investigation from the 1920s onwards. Leonid Vasiliev was perhaps the leading experimental researcher in this field and his studies were conducted on strictly scientific principles under stringent laboratory conditions. They demonstrated that it was possible to declare beyond a reasonable doubt that telepathic transmission could be conducted across vast distances and was not affected by any metallic screening designed to block it. This line of research continued to be practised throughout the existence of the Soviet Union, though with periods of greater and lesser official support.

Stalin also had his own psychic adviser, a Polish Jew named Wolf Messing. In 1937 Messing gave a performance at a theatre in Warsaw, during the course of which he announced that if Hitler invaded Russia it would lead to his death. The Nazis were furious and put a price of 200,000 marks on Messing's head. When they conquered Poland in 1939 Messing was arrested but while he was held in custody he managed to hypnotize all the prison staff, including the governor, and assembled them in his cell. He suggested to them hypnotically that diamonds were hidden in the floor of his cell and he managed by this auto-suggestion to persuade the guards to begin searching for the gems.

As they continued their quest for the imaginary diamonds Messing walked out of the cell and closed the door behind him. Concealing himself in a hay wagon he managed to escape to the USSR. On his arrival he promptly applied to the Ministry of Culture for a job but was rejected. He responded by giving a demonstration of his powers and the Ministry changed its mind. For a year he toured Russia giving public performances.

Within a year he had come to the attention of Stalin who recruited him after subjecting him to some very strenuous tests. Not long after this he announced that 'Soviet tanks will roll into Berlin'. At the time the two countries were close allies and Messing's prediction was an extremely risky one to make. The Germans protested but the Russian authorities replied that they could not be held responsible for his prophecies. In 1943 he made another prediction to a large crowd at a theatre in Novosibirsk that the war would end in May 1945.

The Soviets are rumoured to have made use of Vasiliev's techniques of telepathic hypnotic influence at a distance but no concrete facts have emerged about such activities. Vasiliev's experiments showed that imaginative visualization – exactly the same technique used by many occultists – produced the most successful results.

AMERICA'S USE OF HYPNOTISM AND REMOTE VIEWING

The Americans had been interested in the possibilities of hypnotism ever since their entry into the First World War. Following the Japanese attack on Pearl Harbor, the US Department of War summoned Dr George Estabrooks to advise it on the possible military application of hypnosis. As a result of his advice, American soldiers were hypnotized into losing their fear of death and overcoming their reluctance to kill. More exotic experiments in the uses of hypnotism were also undertaken, including inducing amnesia and employing indirect methods of 'mind control'.

Wolf Messing was Stalin's own psychic adviser. He was arrested by the Nazis in Poland, but escaped by hypnotizing the prison staff and sauntering to freedom.

The Americans also became extremely interested in remote viewing as an espionage tool. Fortune's disciples had attempted this in Britain and psychics in the US soon found themselves being recruited into similar projects. The Office of Strategic Services (OSS), the forerunner of the CIA, was in charge of this and similar undertakings and much effort was devoted to its possible uses.

THE PHILADELPHIA EXPERIMENT

Perhaps the most bizarre project carried out by the US during the war was the so-called Philadelphia Experiment. There are several versions of this story and many of them are little more than exercises in mythmaking. The most credible account is that the US Navy attempted to dematerialize one of its own submarines using a magnetic field in the form of a Möbius strip. This is a single-sided geometrical figure without a beginning or an end, which was allegedly cut in half with an electronic device. Following this action the submarine is said to have vanished from Philadelphia and to have instantaneously appeared in Newport. A more widespread but less plausible story suggests that the US Navy destroyer USS *Eldridge* was dematerialized.

Layers of myth, exaggeration, fabrication and conspiracy theories have been added to the basic story over the course of time. There is no doubt that the Americans carried out experiments of this nature but how large a grain of truth resides within the mountain of mystification surrounding the story will probably never be known.

One of the more surprising facts about the Second World War is that psychic and occult experiments were carried out on a large scale by the British, Americans and Russians as well as the Germans. To paraphrase Churchill, perhaps never in the field of human conflict has so much time and money been wasted on projects delivering so little result.

CONCLUSION

Many writers on the topic of Nazi occultism have fallen into one of two extremes. Some sensationalize trivial events, exaggerate the extent to which occult factors influenced the thinking and actions of Hitler and his associates, present their undoubtedly distorted view of reality as evidence of conscious Satanism and even invent stories out of whole cloth. Others deny that occult considerations played any part in Nazi thinking. They downplay, ignore or dismiss clear evidence that it did play a part, adopt an attitude of superiority and condescension towards those who even mention these events and in general treat Hitler and the Nazis as a phenomenon that is entirely explicable on economic, psychological, structural or other rational grounds alone.

. The rejection of rationality by Hitler was open, contemptuous and total. Those who point to his condemnation of *völkisch* fantasies forget that not only did he condemn rationalism and science with equal vigour but he was also one of the greatest liars ever to hold high office. They also quote selectively and ignore the context of his remarks.

The most reputable accounts of the 'occult Reich' have been given by Francis King, James Webb and Dusty Sklar. King and Webb are careful to distinguish between fact and fantasy and always err on the side of caution when evaluating material. Sklar is slightly less critical of her sources but still adopts a rationalist perspective. All three writers found clear evidence of Nazi involvement in aspects of the occult.

Hugh Trevor-Roper and Alan Bullock were serious major historians and both were convinced that Hitler and other Nazis were influenced by the occult. They certainly did not fly to the speculative level of some authors on this subject but recognized that occult ideas and practices did play a significant part in the Third Reich.

To assume that occult fantasies were not profoundly influential in Nazi Germany is as mistaken and superficial a view as the notion that Hitler was the leader of a Satanic coven consciously serving those ends. Both of these attitudes are extreme, are contradicted by the facts and positively hinder our understanding of the Third Reich.

Himmler devoted considerable time, effort and money to a whole range of occult endeavours including his neo-pagan festivals, attempts to communicate with Heinrich the Fowler, researching Atlantis, sending expeditions in search of pieces of the supposed fallen moon, studying the magical properties of the bells of Oxford's cathedral and debating the significance of the top hat.

Rosenberg researched Atlantis, the Cathars, German prehistory and Masonic rituals and wanted to replace Christianity with a revived Gnosticism. Goering believed that the earth was hollow and that the space was inhabited by humans. The German Navy wasted large amounts of money paying mediums and dowsers to locate British ships with zero success.

Hitler allowed his entire policy to be dominated by racial fantasies that went far beyond simple prejudice to become a belief system that resembled a science fiction novel rather than a rational political ideology. Anti-Semitism was common in his day but few shared the Nazi leader's belief that Jews were not simply inferior but were literally not human.

Hitler's belief in Hörbiger's Glacial Cosmogony led to astonishing amounts of money being wasted on this scientifically valueless theory, which decisively affected the course of the war. His failure to equip German troops with winter clothing during the invasion of the Soviet Union was based upon Hörbigerian weather forecasts that predicted a mild winter. Thousands of lives were lost needlessly as a result of his preference for an occult cosmology rather than scientific meteorology.

Hitler and the Nazis seized on the German people's longing for a saviour, a renewed sense of pride in their nation and a desire for a common purpose. They took these emotions and distorted them utterly, deceiving their fellow Germans into worshipping a psychopathic dictator and turning national pride into a sense of shame as the German people finally awoke too late to the horrors that had been perpetrated in their name and to the utter perversion of all normal moral values. For twelve astonishing years, Germany turned its back upon rationality and compassion and gave its allegiance to a man and a movement that plumbed new depths of human depravity. The spiritual impulses of millions were perverted into the dark worship of a brutal madman and his irrational vision of the world.

The great religions of the world offer salvation to all true believers. Even political ideologies like Marxism and liberalism make their promise of a better society to every human being irrespective of race, skin colour or gender. Nazism made no such appeal to anyone outside the favoured Nordic group. To the majority of the human race it offered nothing beyond slavery and death.

No society built upon such shallow moral foundations can ever endure. For twelve brief years the world saw what happens when reason, kindness, moderation and fairness are cast aside and a dark fanatical tyranny takes their place. In their desire to become superhuman the Nazis ended by being far less than human. The story of the Third Reich stands as the ultimate warning from history of the results of abandoning the values that define us as human beings.

BIBLIOGRAPHY

Ashe, Geoffrey, *The Ancient Wisdom*, Macmillan, 1977.

Bellamy, H. S., *Moon, Myths and Man*, Faber and Faber, 1949.

Bullock, Alan, *Hitler: A Study in Tyranny*, Odhams, 1952.
   Hitler and Stalin: Parallel Lives, Fontana, 1993.

Cecil, Robert, *The Myth of the Master Race*, Dodd Mead, 1972.

Cohn, Norman, *Warrant for Genocide*, Serif, 1990 (1966).

Cross, Colin, *Hitler*, Hodder & Stoughton, 1973.

Donington, Richard, *Wagner's 'Ring' and its Symbols*, Faber and Faber, 1969.

Evans-Wentz, W. Y., *The Tibetan Book of the Great Liberation*, OUP, 1954.
   Tibetan Yoga and Secret Doctrine, OUP, 1958.

Feder, Gottfried, *The Programme of the NSDAP*, Allen & Unwin, 1934.

Fest, Joachim C., *The Face of the Third Reich*, Weidenfeld & Nicolson, 1970.
   Hitler, Weidenfeld & Nicolson, 1974.

Fischer, Klaus P., *Nazi Germany: A New History*, Constable, 1995.

FitzGerald, Michael, *Adolf Hitler: A Portrait*, Spellmount, 2006.

Frischauer, Willi, *Himmler*, Odhams, 1962.

Golding, Louis, *The Jewish Problem*, Penguin, 1938.

Goodrich-Clarke, Nicholas, *The Occult Roots of Nazism*, Taurus Parke, 2005.

Grant, Madison, *The Passing of the Great Race*, Lulu.com, 2011 (1916).

Heinsch, J., *Principles of Prehistoric Sacred Geography*, Zodiac House, 1991 (1938).

Herzstein, Robert Edwin, *The War That Hitler Won: Nazi Propaganda*, Hamish Hamilton, 1979.

Hitler, Adolf, *Mein Kampf*, Hurst and Blackett, 1939.

Jung, Emma and Marie-Louise von Frantz, *The Grail Legend*, Hodder, 1970.

Kershaw, Ian, *Hitler 1889–1936: Hubris*, Allen Lane, 1998.
    Hitler 1936–1945: Nemesis, Allen Lane, 2000.

Kersten, Felix, *The Kersten Memoirs*, Hutchinson, 1956.

King, Francis, *Satan and Swastika*, Mayflower, 1976.

Kubizek, August, *Young Hitler: The Story of Our Friendship*, Allen Wingate, 1954.

Levenda, Peter, *Unholy Alliance*, Continuum, 2002.

Liebenfels, Jörg Lanz von [Adolf Lanz], *Theozoology*, Europa House, 2004 (1905).

List, Guido von, *The Secret of the Runes*, Destiny Books, 1988 (1908).

Maclellan, Alec, *The Lost World of Agharti*, Corgi, 1982.

Magre, Maurice, *The Return of the Magi*, Sphere, 1975 (1931).

Maraini, Fosco, *Secret Tibet*, Hutchinson, 1952.

Maser, Werner, *Hitler*, Allen Lane, 1973.

Nichols, Ross, *Seasons at War*, Forge Press, 1947.

Ossendowski, Ferdinand, *Men, Beasts and Gods*, Edward Arnold, 1923.

Padfield, Peter, *Himmler: Reichsführer SS*, Macmillan, 1990.

Poliakov, Leon, *The Aryan Myth*, Basic Books, 1974.

Postone, Moishe, *Anti-Semitism and National Socialism*, Chronos, 2000.

Rauschning, Hermann, *Hitler Speaks*, Thornton Butterworth, 1939.
    Germany's Revolution of Destruction, Heinemann, 1939.

Reichmann, Eva G., *Hostages of Civilisation: The Social Sources of National Socialist Anti-Semitism*, Gollancz, 1950.

Roberts, Stephen H., *The House that Hitler Built*, Methuen, 1937.

Roerich, George N., *Trails to Inmost Asia*, Yale University Press, 1931.

Roerich, Nicholas, *Altai-Himalayas*, Jarrolds, 1930.
    Himalayas, Abode of Light, David Marlowe, 1947.

Rosenberg, Alfred, *Selected Writings*, Jonathan Cape, 1960.
    Memoirs, Ziff-Davis, 1949.
Schauberger, Viktor, *The Water Wizard*, Gateway Books, 1998.
Schellenberg, Walter, *Memoirs*, André Deutsch, 1956.
Scrutton, Robert, *The Other Atlantis*, Sphere, 1977.
Shirer, William S., *The Nightmare Years 1930–1940*, Little, Brown, 1984.
    The Rise and Fall of the Third Reich, Gallery, 2000 (1950).
Sklar, Dusty, *The Nazis and the Occult*, Dorset Press, 1977.
Smelser, Ronald, *Robert Ley: Hitler's Labour Front Leader*, Berg, 1992.
Spence, Lewis, *Will Europe Follow Atlantis?*, Rider, 1942.
    Occult Causes of the Present War, Kessinger, 1998 (1939).
Stern, J. P., *Hitler: The Führer and the People*, Fontana, 1975.
Taylor, Brendan and Wilfried van de Will, *The Nazification of Art*, Winchester Press, 1990.
Teeling, William, *Why Britain Prospers*, Right Book Club, 1938.
Toland, John, *Adolf Hitler*, Doubleday, 1976.
Tolischus, Otto D., *They Wanted War*, Hamish Hamilton, 1940.
Tomas, Andrew, *Atlantis: From Legend to Discovery*, Robert Hale, 1972.
    Shambhala: Oasis of Light, Sphere, 1977.
Trevor-Roper, Hugh, *The Last Days of Hitler*, Macmillan, 1947.
Webb, James, *The Occult Establishment*, Richard Drew, 1981.
Weininger, Otto, *Sex and Character*, Heinemann, 1906.
Whitford, Alan, *Unemployment and the Nazi Revolution*, Barnet Unemployed Group, 1986.
Wishaw, E. M., *Atlantis in Andalusia*, Rider, 1929.
Wohl, Louis de, *The Stars of Peace and War*, Rider, 1952.
Wrench, Evelyn, *I Loved Germany*, Michael Joseph, 1940.

INDEX

PICTURE CREDITS